BEGINNER'S GUIDE TO SERGER

Amy Bardot

TABLE OF CONTENTS

INTRODUCTION

Is it your first time to use a serger? This is an absolute beginner's guide that will teach you step-by-step basics on the use of a serger machine.

A serger machine is the most preferred sewing machine compared to a regular sewing machine due to its versatile uses. You can use this machine to create different types of stitches, seam fabrics while at the same time overcasting the raw edges, adding finishings, trimming edges, and sewing decorates stitches to your fabric.

A serger machine uses multiple threads to seam your fabric making the stitches more strong than those of a regular sewing machine. It gives your garment a neat and professional finishing.

In this tutorial, you will learn how to look for a good serger machine for your next sewing projects and some of the best serging machines in the market.

You will also learn how to set up your serger machines, the different parts of your machines, how each of the parts operates, and their functions.

Before you begin your first serging project, you need to learn how to thread your machine like a pro. In addition, you will be able to adjust your machine settings to ensure you have a perfect stitch for your projects. Depending on the type of fabric, you will know how to adjust the stitch length and needle tensions to create a balance.

Knowing all these essential techniques, then you're ready to begin your serging journey. You will be able to make a variety of custom made clothing and other accessories for you and your family!

With just the basics on how to operate the machine, you will be able to make your garment finishing like a pro. And with time, the serger will be the most useful tool in your sewing room.

CHAPTER ONE

Parts Of A Serger

Have you ever wondered how those perfectly stitch finishing on garments is done? Well, you can also add this professional finishing to your projects or garments. All you need is a Serger machine.

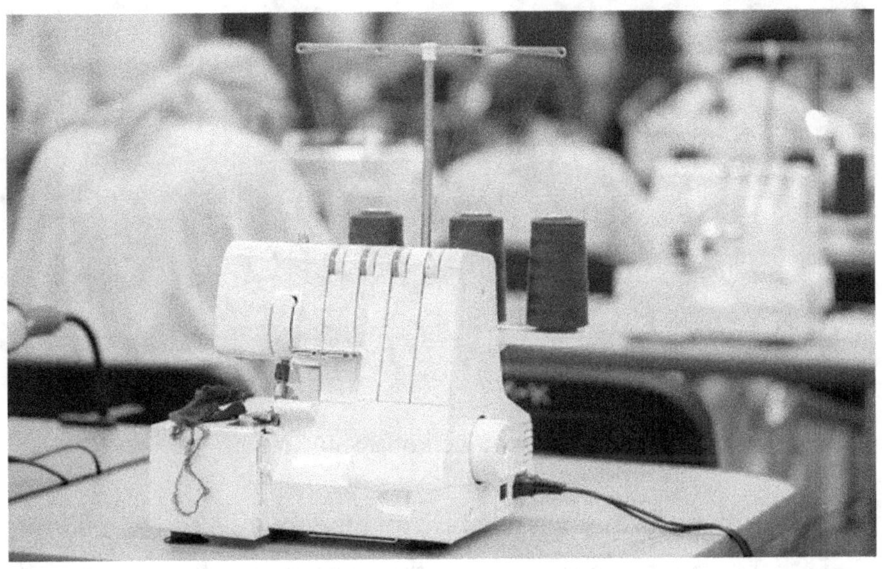

Image source: Andy Shell/Shutterstock

In this guide, I will walk you through all the essentials you need to know about the serger.

To start with, you need to know your serger, so in this chapter, you will learn about the serge, how to use it, and different parts of a serger. By the time we wrap up, you will be sewing with confidence!

What is a Serger?

A serger or overlock machine is a special sewing machine that trims the edges of the fabric, overcast it, and sews a seam around the fabric. It can also sew tightly rolled hems or bind fabrics together using an overlock stitch. You should not confuse it with a sewing machine. Both machines sew stitches but they do so differently.

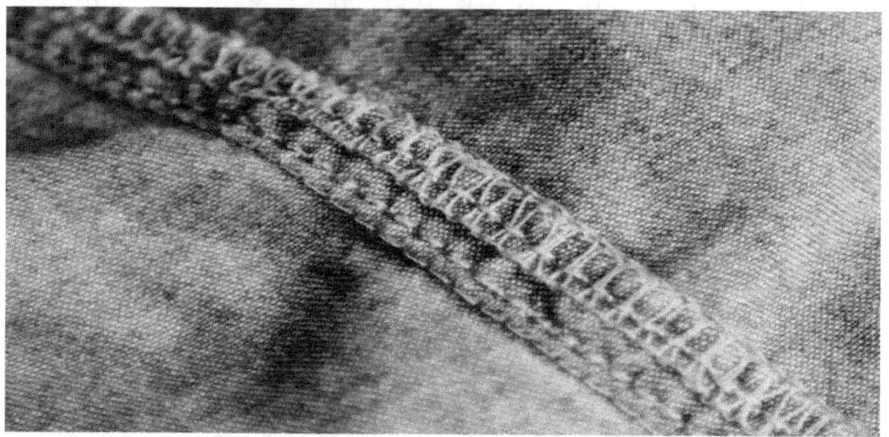

Image source: Keikona/Shutterstock

The serger not only binds fabric together but it also has a cutting blade that cuts the excess fabric at the same time. The cutting blade sits right before the needle unlike the normal sewing machine, you have to cut your project before sewing. As a result, it saves you time and at the same time sews clean and tidy seams.

A normal sewing machine uses only one thread to sew or two in case you have a double-needle machine. While a serger uses 3 to 4 threads to create interlocking stitches.

I personally prefer a serger machine to a sewing machine because it makes your sewing tasks much easier and faster. You don't have to spend more of your sewing time doing the unnecessary work associated with the sewing machine.

The stitches are better and strong especially if you're sewing children's clothes. In addition, you can use special stitches to make your garment look more attractive.

Why you need a serger

- A serger machine is a must-have if you love sewing stretchy fabrics, fleece, knits, and sweatshirt fabrics
- If you want to create a seam and an overlock stitch at once. When you want to cut the edges of the fabric as you sew, you can use the serger machine because it gives you clean raw edges.
- If you want to use thicker threads to create decorative edges.
- A serger is much faster and easier than a sewing machine.
- A serger gives you better, stronger, and durable stitches
- When you want to create rolled hems on your sheer fabric and other lightweight materials.
- When you want to use elastic threads, beading wires, cords, and pearls to serge the raw edges of your garment and have a beautiful finishing.
- If you want to add zippers to custom made pillows and simple bags.
- When you want to speed up your sewing and create gathering stitches much faster.
- If you want to prevent raveling of fabrics. The serger adds professional finishing to the raw edges of your fabric.

Parts of a Serger

Before you start using a serger, you need to know the different parts that make this machine. Look up at the handbook that comes with your new machine and make sure you can identify them.

Learning these parts of the serger will help you to achieve an excellent finish of your garments.

Although the sergers are different based on the model, most of them have similar parts.

Each serger has a vertical pole and a horizontal rod fixed at the top. There are several evenly distributed holes where threads are fed through. Below are spool pins that hold the thread. Each spool of thread has a tension control.

Some Sergers have a presser foot while others have a level to lift and lower the foot. On the right side of the needle, there is a blade that cuts excess clothing as you sew.

There are sergers with fabric catcher, a little box that is used to hold the pieces of the cut fabric.

Let's have a look at the main parts of the serger sewing machine. They include;

Parts of a Serger

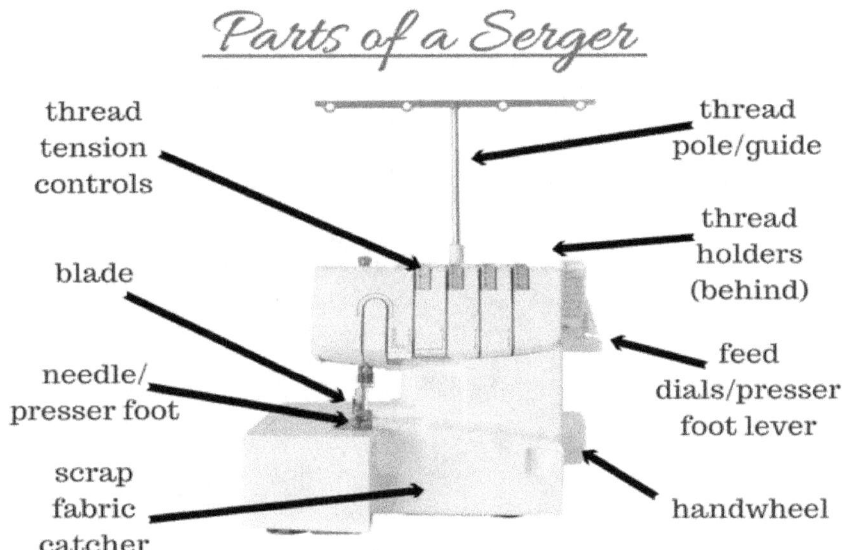

Image source: Serger manual

1. Tension dials: Tension dials help in balancing your stitch. It ensures you sew smooth stitches without any loops. Just like tension dials in a conventional sewing machine, you can adjust the tension dial on each of the threads in a serger and have a perfect stitch. It works well in coordination with other parts of the machine to give you an appropriate stitch based on the type of fabric you're using.

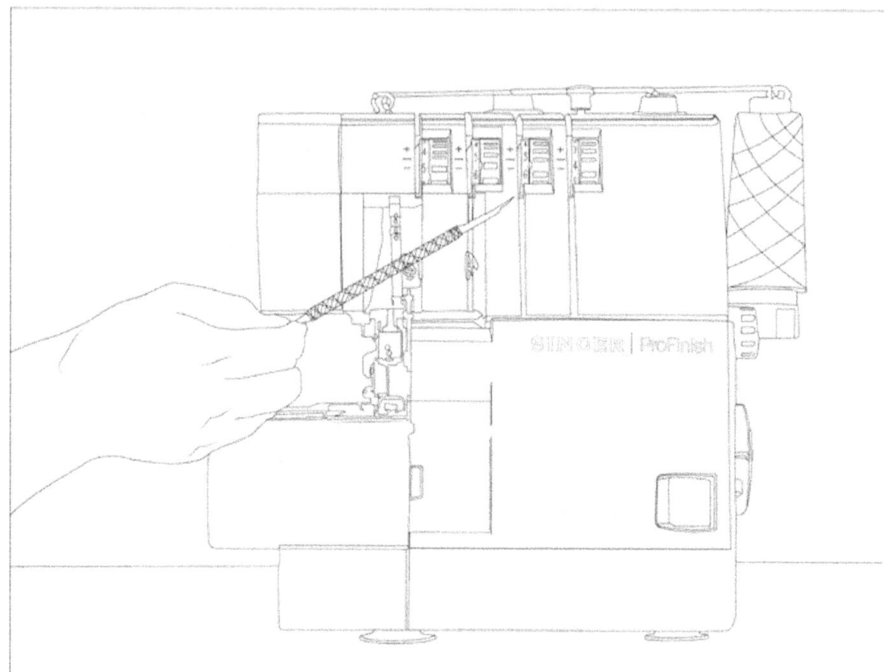

Therefore, you should set your tension dial based on the weight of the fabric or project.

A balanced stitch has the upper and lower looper meet at the edge of the fabric while at the same time there is no pucker or gape of the needle threads.

When tension is very high, there will be too much friction on thread leading to a tight sew and the machine will keep pulling the thread. So you need to adjust the tension to achieve a perfect balance in all the threads.

2. Loopers: Loopers are used to create stitches instead of using a bobbin. There are two types of loopers: the upper and lower looper. The stitches are created through the locking of the needle thread and the looper. It also uses the same mechanism to create finish

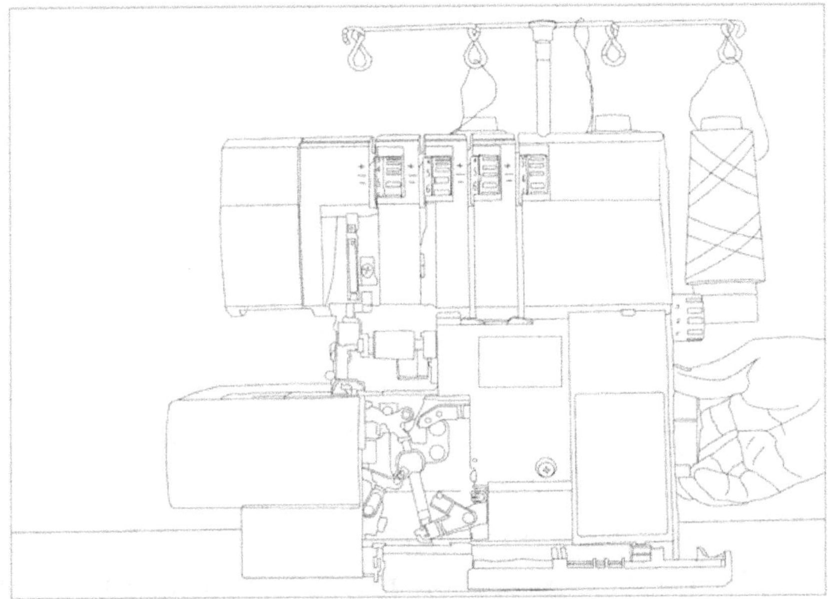

Looper threads do not penetrate the fabric but they do affect each other as you sew.

If your looper's threads do not meet at the fabric edges, this means one of the threads is pulled to the wrong side.

For example, if the upper looper tension is loose or the lower looper tension is very tight then you will have the upper looper pulled to the wrong side (bottom of the fabric). To correct this, you need to do proper adjustments based on the stitches affected.

This also applies to the lower looper thread. If the upper looper tension is tight while the lower looper tension is loose, then the lower looper thread is pulled to the right side or top of the fabric.

3. **Feed system:** This consists of the feed dog, a needle plate, and a presser foot. Feed dogs look like some jagged metal teeth and

they're located on the stitch plate which is below the pressure foot.

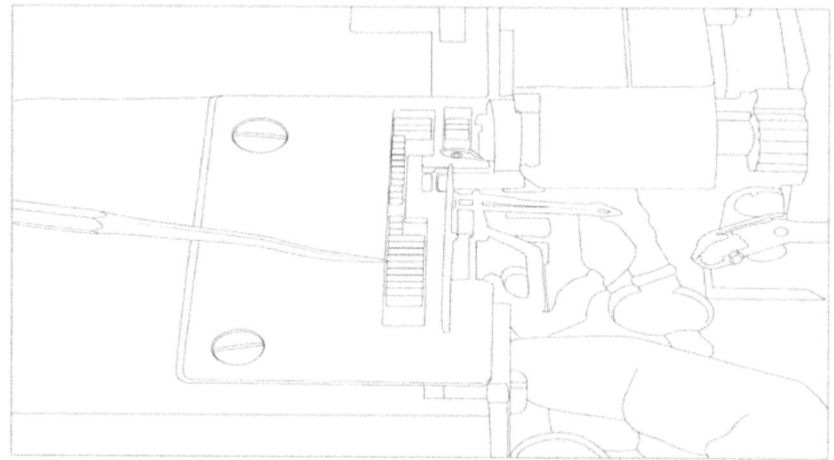

These feed systems work together to ensure the fabric is fed evenly through the serger. Some machines do have two different feed dogs which help prevent stretched seams.

4. **Stitch fingers:** It resembles a figure like shape and it is located close to the cutting blade and at the right side of the pressure foot. It acts as the center point for threads going through the serger and guides each thread to create a stitch on the fabric edges.

Threads pass through the stitch finger when sewing and come off through the back of the pressure foot.

In some brands, stitch finger is called stitch former and it works well in conjunction with pressure foot, needles, and threads.

5. **Cutting system:** It uses a movable upper knife to trim seam allowances while at the same time the lower knife remains stationary. The two knives work together in a coordinating manner and move at the same speed as that of the needles.

6. **3-4 thread spools:** Thread spools are designed to hold 2000 – 3000 yards of thread. In most cases, the threads are used in multiple of two or more spools. They are located at the back or at the top of the machine. Larger machines have more thread spools.

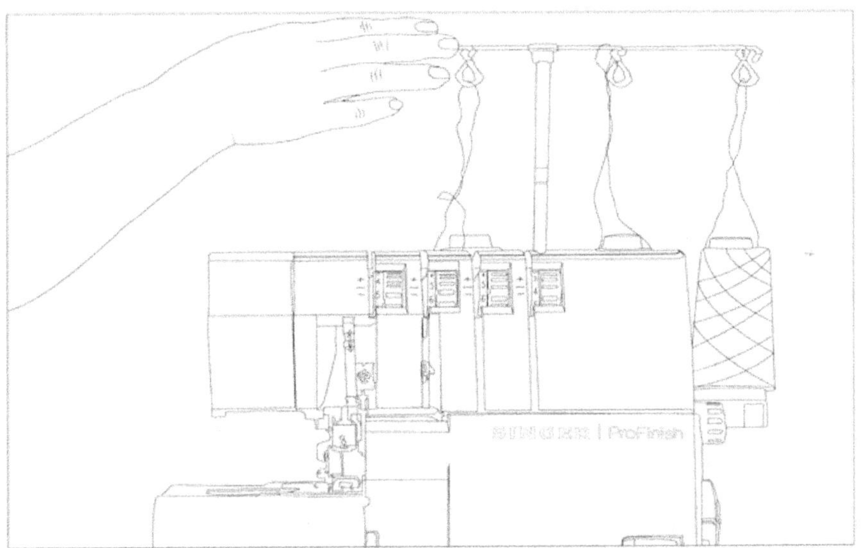

7. **2 needles:** A serger has two needles that have different heights when inserted into the sewing machine. The left needle is at a higher level than the right needle. Some old sergers only come with one needle while modern sergers have two needles.

You can remove one of the needles and work with one but the serger will still function with three threads in both cases.

If you're using 4 thread stitching, then you should adjust the thread tensions of the two needles. If you're using 3 thread stitching, you only adjust one needle thread tension.

If you want to replace the needles, you need to unscrew the clamp screws that hold each needle and dispose of the old needle.

Insert the new needle by pushing it deep into the slot. Make sure the shank flat side faces the front and then screw the clamp screw back into its position. Now test your serger machine.

8. **Stitch Length:** When starting up with your sewing, you don't think much about the stitch length. Most probably, you will use the default stitch length already set by the manufacturer.

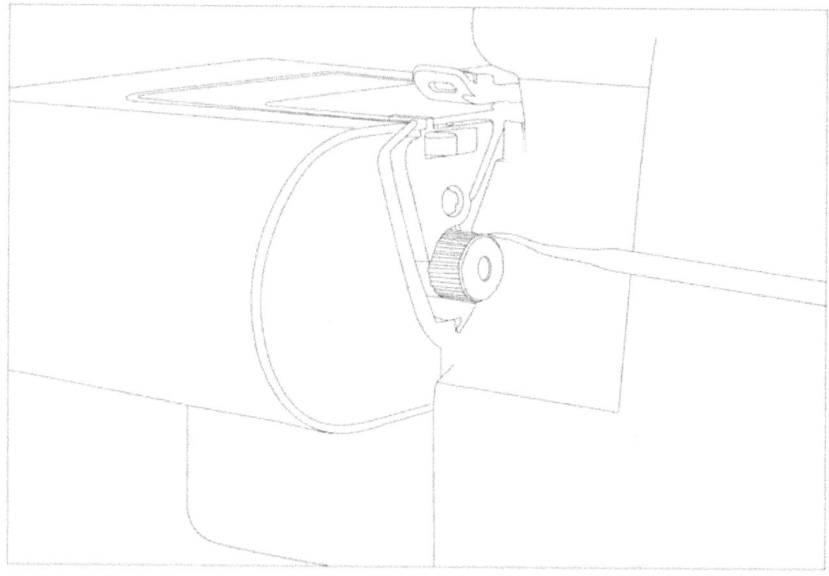

Default stitch length works for most beginner projects although this depends on what you're sewing.

But as you continue sewing more projects, you will need varying stitch length that suits the fabric and also the purpose of the stitch. To adjust how long each stitch is sewn, you need to adjust the feed dogs. Feed dogs control how much fabric is to be pulled by each stitch. If you need a longer stitch, then more fabric needs to be pulled through.

9.　　**A pressing feet:** Different presser feet helps you increase efficiency and better results in your project. These different serger feet makes it easy to achieve the specialty stitches and various sewing techniques .

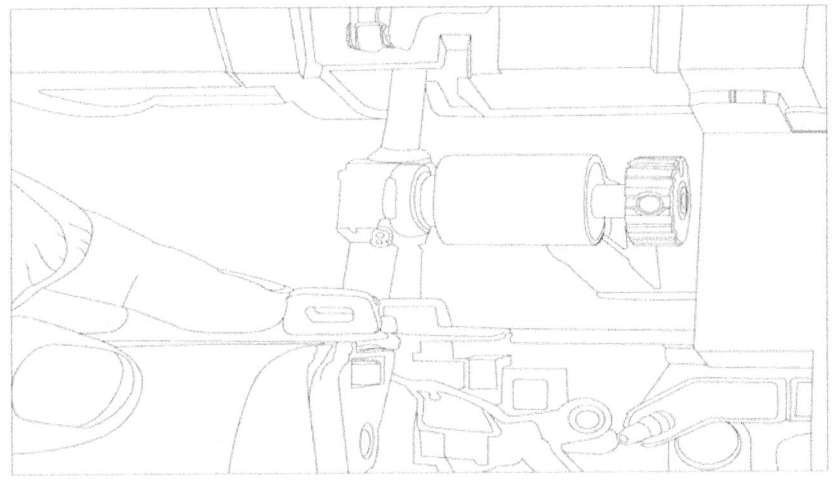

Although you're required to match the serger feet based on your serger brand and model, you can also interchange them.

The parts combine together to do multiple stitches simultaneously. For example, when you want to sew a fabric the feed dog ensures it is evenly fed through the serger, and then moves the fabric until the knives trim all the edges. The loopers and the needles sew the stitches on the fabric and then it is fed off the stitch fingers behind the needle.

In the end, you will have a professional finished edge of the fabric. The fabric can either be a garment or any home décor project.

Serger Feet

A serger foot can be part of your overlock machine or you can buy them as accessories. There are different types of serger feet.

The feet act as an attachment that enables the serger to create different forms of stitches when the fabric moves over the feed dogs. That is, it ensures thread is wrapped around the edges of the fabric to avoid unraveling.

The feet consist of:

Elastic/tape foot: Used for adding an elastic or sewing tape to your garment.

Blind hem foot/ blind stitch foot: Used for sewing seams on skirts and trousers so that they remain hidden. You can also sew cuffs on a knit fabric using this blind stitch foot.

Shirring foot: It is used to create gathers in your fabric

Pearl/Sequin foot/beading foot: This is ideal for sewing pearls, sequins, and beans on the garment.

Piping /Cording foot: It is ideal for sewing piping on your garment. It also has a groove where the piping or the cording passes through and attaches to the garment.

Lace foot: It enables you to add laces and ribbons at the edges of the fabric.

Gimp/ Yarn application tool: This tool is suitable for attaching a thin thread or a wire at the cut edges of the fabric.

Functions of a serger

A serger or overlock machine can help you in;

· Sewing seams on knit fabrics

· Finish the seams on a fabric

· Sew rolled hems and edges

· Gathering

How a Serger Works

This special sewing machine performs multiple functions simultaneously to create a strong stitch.

When you want to sew a garment, the fabric is first fed to your machine through the feed dog. Then the fabric moves along as the knife trims the edges. After trimming, the loopers and needles sew stitches at the fabric edges, then the fabric is forwarded to the stitch finger behind the needle.

The machine repeats the same process for the next stitch until you're able to add a professional finish to your garment. However, for you to achieve this professional finishing, you need to know how to guide the fabric through the serger machine.

Once you're able to learn how the machine works, you will be ready to dive in and start sewing more projects.

Chapter Summary

Before starting any sewing project, you need to first learn about your serger and how it sews. If you have been using a standard sewing machine, it will be much easier to learn how to use the serger.

You need to identify the different parts of the serger machine. This is because the threading and thread tension in a serger machine is different from that of a standard sewing machine.

A serger machine will cut some of the seam allowances in the fabric as you sew, thus saving you a lot of time.

In the next chapter, you will learn sewing tools and their uses.

CHAPTER TWO

Tools For Operating A Serger

There are a lot of sewing resources and supplies over the internet and probably wondering where do I begin?

If you're a beginner, it can be very overwhelming for you to choose the best sewing tools and equipment. While some of the sewing tools are a must-have, others are optional.

To help you solve your dilemma on sewing tools, I have put together some of the tools you need to start your sewing!

Also, you will be able to learn the work of each of the tools.

With this guide, you can determine what tools you need to buy before you go to your local supply store.

Have you ever walked to any sewing supplier store? Most stores have multiple sewing tools ranging from simple screwdrivers to other sophisticated equipment. That alone can leave you nervous if you're a beginner.

With this list, no more dilemma on what to buy. With the basic sewing tools, you're set to sew   .

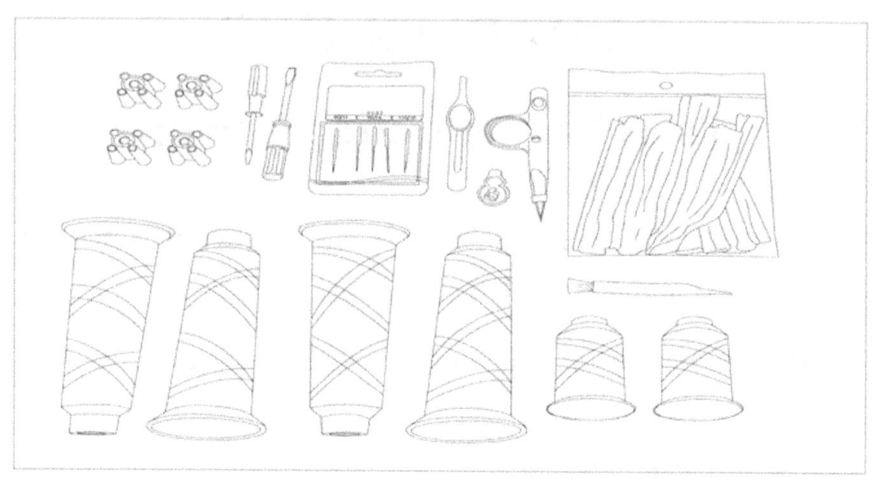

Basic Serger sewing tools

If you're on a budget, get these basic sewing tools and learn how to use each one of them correctly! They will get you started as well as help you complete a simple sewing project.

1. Screwdriver: This one of the most important tools for a tailor. It is used to change the needles or unscrew some hidden parts of your overlock machine that need to be cleaned or fixed.

2. Serger needles: There are types of needle brands that are compatible with certain brands of a serger. You can find some of these universal serger needles for your machine.

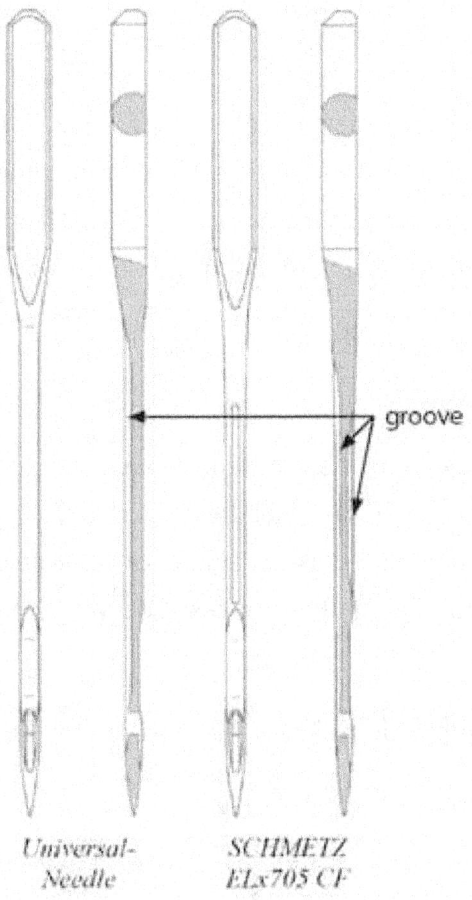

Other serger manufacturers recommend using certain types of needle brands. You may consider this option when shopping for needles for your machine. So choose your favorite brand of needles and go ahead to install it in your machine.

Different needles have different shank shapes. Some sergers use round-shaped shank needles while newer models have a flat shank. Needle shank thickness and size also vary. Therefore, using the recommended brand on a particular serger model will ensure it fits well.

Some types of sergers can still use the regular sewing needle although this depends on the model of the serger.

When inserting the new needle, always make sure it fits the same as if you're installing it in a regular sewing machine. If after fixing the needle doesn't fit well or not creating stitches as it is expected, then stick with the recommended brand on the user manual.

Always remember the right needle should extend down lower than the left needle.

3. **Needle inserter:** This is a must-have tool in your sewing list. Needle inserters easily hold needles when inserting in your sewing machine. It helps you to easily replace or remove serger needles. It has an ergonomic handle that makes it easy to use and comfortable on your hands.

All you need to do is insert the needle into the needle inserter, fix it in your serger machine, and then tighten the clamp screws.

4. **Needle threader:** A needle threader helps you to easily insert the thread in the needle. You don't have all your projects delayed because you couldn't get the needle threaded. The threader works with all types of needles.

5. **Tweezers:** These are used to pick small objects that you can't pick with your fingers or reach to places with limited spaces. Keep one or two of these tweezers in your accessory box. With a tweezer, you can remove unwanted threads, reach the lower looper, insert needles in your machine, do beading, and do general crafts.

The curved shape of the tweezers makes threading very easy when using your overlock machine.

6. **Thread nippers:** Thread nipper is another must-have tool in your accessory kit. This tool is essential in craft projects that require more accuracy. In this case, the large scissors are inefficient.

Therefore, thread nippers can be of great help in cutting unwanted threads in a garment while being keen on the clothes details. If your cloth or garment has some detailed craft, then thread nippers will help make it neat by removing or cutting unwanted pieces or small nips.

7. **Tiny lint brush:** After hours of sewing, removing lint, and cleaning your machine is very important. Therefore, the lint brush is great for the maintenance of your sewing machine.

This tiny lint brush can clean those small spots or hard to reach parts of the serger machine.

8. **Spool net:** Spool nets are used to keep your threads neat, you don't have to waste your time sorting through a mess of entangled threads.

If you're using a transparent nylon thread that winds off, you can put your thread inside the spool net. If the spool net is long, you can fold it to fit the size of the spool. This ensures your thread remains neat.

A spool net tightens the upper thread tension therefore, you should adjust the upper thread tension to accommodate the spool net.

9.   **4 spool holders:** A spool holder or spool cap is used to hold the spool on the pin. The spool cap ensures the thread is in place and your spool doesn't come off the pin as you sew. It also ensures the thread doesn't snag on the spool.

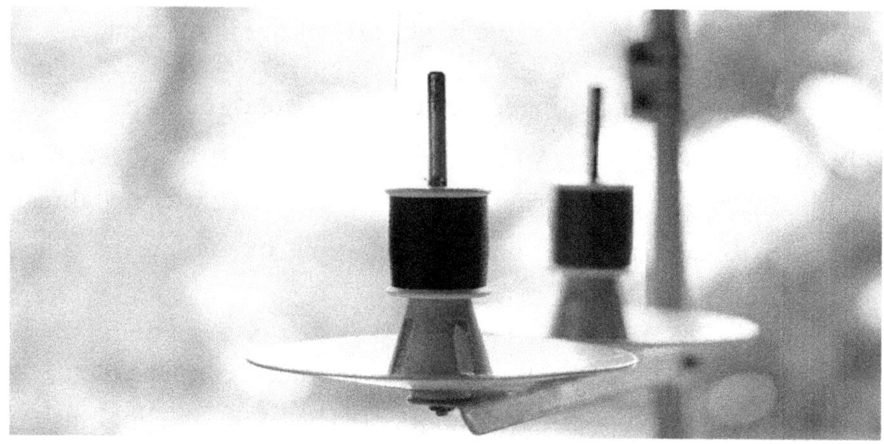

Image source: FaiPloypilin/Shutterstock

The spool cap shouldn't hold the thread tightly on the spool pin. The spool needs enough space so that it could rotate on the spool pin as the thread is pulled on the spool.

10. **Thread spool holder:** This acts as a stand for the spools of your sewing thread. These spools are mounted on the pins such that they can rotate freely when the thread is unwound.

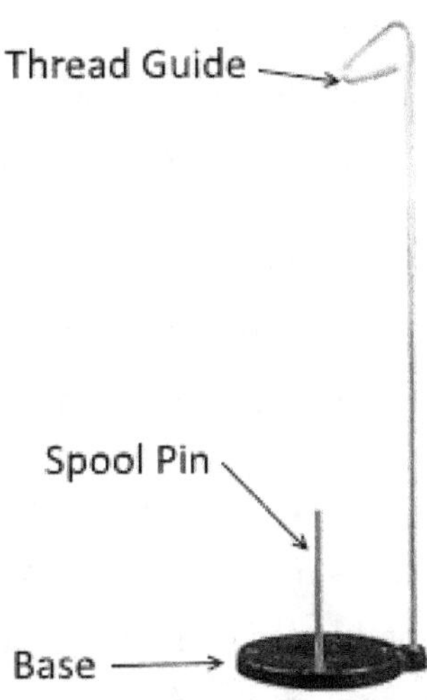

Image source: Serger manual

There is a wide variety of threads in the market and depending on how the threads are packaged, a spool pin cannot accommodate a larger thread. Therefore, in such cases, you need a stand for your thread cones and spools (thread spool holder).

11. **Rolled Hem presser foot:** It is also called the narrow hem foot and it is used when sewing a narrow hem. The foot helps in folding the edges of the fabric before it passes through the needle. This ensures you have a professional finish of your garment.

You can use a rolled hem foot when working with light and medium weight fabrics.

The rolled hem technique ensures all the finishes of the seam allowances are inside the hem.

12. **Upper knife & lower Knife:** Knives or cutting blades play a huge role in using a serger machine. The knives trim the edges of the fabric before sewing stitches. This results in a neat finished edge.

The upper and lower knives work together to trim the fabric during stitching. The upper blade usually moves up and down while the lower blade remains stationary under the needle plate.

You can disengage the upper blade if you want decorative sewing or when you don't want to cut the fabric when stitching. For example, disengaging the blades can help you use elastic, topstitch, or any other decorative stitch at the edges of the fabric.

The blades ensure you have a neat and professional-looking garment. You don't have to spend more time going back to trim the seam.

If you're planning to remove or replace the blades, make sure to disconnect the serger from the network. To remove the upper blade, unscrew it and pull it out.

The lower knife is fixed with a screw that has a special washer and to remove it, you have to loosen the screws. Although this depends on the model of your serger machine.

13. **Awl or stiletto:** This is a pointed tool that allows you to feed your fabric next to the cutting blade and close to the presser foot. The awl will keep your fabric moving on areas you can't touch with your fingers.

14. **Wonder clips by clover:** If you have been sewing over the pins you're your sewing machine, it can be challenging when using

a serger machine. If you serge over the pins, you can damage your knives. Instead of using pins that can cause an accident, you can hold your fabrics with wonder clip to avoid these problems.

How to use serger needles

Serge needles have sharp points that allow them to sew any type of fabric. Ballpoint needles are highly recommended by manufacturers when sewing performing knits. This is because the needles do not pierce the fabric instead, it goes in between the thread when sewing.

These needles have a groove both at the front and at the backside of the blade to reduce the number of skipped stitches. The long groove helps create chain stitches on a piece of fabric.

Older models of sergers have one needle while modern sergers come with two needles. You can also remove one, although this is optional.

Inserting new needles

When inserting the needles in your machine, they should not be parallel with each other. The left needle should sit higher than the right needle.

The serger has two needle clamps screws to hold each of the needles. Therefore, you have to unscrew the needle clamp and remove the old needle. Ensure the used needle is well disposed of.

Insert the new needle by pushing its shank deep into the needle slot. The flat side of the needle shank should face the front. Screw the clamp screws back in place and test.

Tips on working with needles

Before replacing the needles in your serger machine, ensure you have the right length. Different machines use different needle lengths so confirm with your serger manual the recommended needle length or number.

In addition, the size of the needle you choose should be suitable for the fabric you want to sew and the thread size you will use. Your sewing manual has an operator manual chart that highlights different needle sizes and recommended thread sizes for different types of fabrics. You can also get the manual from a reputable website.

Using a larger diameter needle for a thin fabric will result in an unattractive stitch with big needle holes left on the fabric. So always make sure you use the right needle size based on the fabric type.

Also, make sure the needle is inserted straight and doesn't have any burr or dull point.

When sewing special fabrics, choose the right needle for that. For example, use ballpoint needles when you want to sew knits and a wedge needle when you want to sew leather fabrics.

Parts of a needle

Needle plate/Throat plate: Some manufacturers of certain models do recommend using a needle plate with an elongated hole to serge zig-zag stitches and a round hole when serging straight stitches.

Using the wrong needle plate may result in skipped stitches when serging straight stitches. This mostly happens when sewing synthetic fabrics.

· **Feed dog:** This a metal bar with diagonal teeth that emerges above the hole on the throat plate. It moves back and forth in between the needle plate and pulls (feed) the fabric in your sewing machine before the needle makes the next stitch.

Adjust the setting such that the needle creates a seam with 10 to 12 stitches. If you're sewing a thin fabric, then a short stitch of 14 – 16 per inch is more desirable. Leather and vinyl fabrics require a long stitch of about 6-10 stitches for each inch of the seam

· **Presser foot:** Your presser foot should have enough pressure for holding the fabric on the feed dog in order to make uniform stitches. If you're sewing a heavy fabric, then light pressure will be used to pull the fabric. Pulling the inner pin will increase the pressure while releasing the outer ring reduces the pressure.

A roller-type presser foot can give you better feeding results than the standard pressure foot when sewing with vinyl fabric, velvet, loosely knit, or slippery fabric.

Read your model instruction manual to know more about how to change the settings of the presser foot.

· **Thread tension:** To obtain a perfect stitch, you have to adjust the upper and lower tension dials. Different machines have the upper tension located in different areas. Some machines may have it located on the upper arm of the machine head, on the faceplate, or at the front of the needle bar.

The lower tension dial is located on a bobbin case or on the shuttle. Just adjust the screw near the center of the spring holding the tension.

Lower tension adjustment

If you had removed the lower tension spring while cleaning, or changed the adjustment, then follow the normal adjustment procedure just like adjusting an ordinary sewing machine. In most cases, you have to assume the lower tension is correct unless proven wrong. You should make the adjustments on the upper tension.

If there were initial changes on the lower tension, then set the lower and upper tension such that there is a slight drag in each of the threads. Make sure the bobbin and spool have the same size of thread. After adjusting the tension, test the machine to see the stitch size formed. You can use different colors for the bobbin and spool for you to see the stitches clearly. Adjust the stitch length control to sew medium stitch length. Test the stitches again on a piece of cloth.

In a perfect stitch, threads should lock at the center or halfway between the layers of the cloth. There should be no loops formed at the top or bottom of the seam. If the top side of the seam forms a loop while the top thread remains straight, then you should loosen the upper tension thread because it is tighter than the lower tension thread. However, if the loop on the spool thread appears on the bottom of the seam and the lower thread remains straight, then you should tighten the upper thread.

How to choose the Best Serger

Looking for a new Serger can be a bit overwhelming with so many brands and models in the market. If you're new to the sewing world you may wonder what to look for and how to choose the best serger machine for your sewing projects.

Don't worry anymore. This guide will help in choosing the best serger machine.

Before you buy the serger you need to:

Determine your sewing needs

Features to look for (how often do you sew? Do you have eyesight issues? What kind of fabric do you sew?)

Sergers based on your sewing needs

Serger machines based on the needs of customers are classified into three:

1.   Basic serger machines
2.   Experimental serger machines
3.   Automatic serger machines

Before you select the serger model to buy, ask yourself what kind of a tailor are you?

1.   Do you need a basic serger to create professional finishing to the edges of a fabric? Do you use light or medium weight fabrics in your sewing projects?
2.   Do you love experimenting with different types of fabrics? Do you like to practice sewing with woven fabrics, thick fabrics, and

stretchy knits? Do you stitch athletic flatlock on sportswear? Or do you stitch rolled hems on a chiffon dress?

3. Looking for the easiest serger in the market? Do you struggle with threading and choosing the right settings to adjust the tension dial?

Whichever kind of tailor you are, there are different serger machines designed to handle different tasks. Let's have a look at these machines based on the above options

1. Basic serger machine

If you're able to answer yes to questions in number 1, then you need a simple budget-friendly serger machine   .

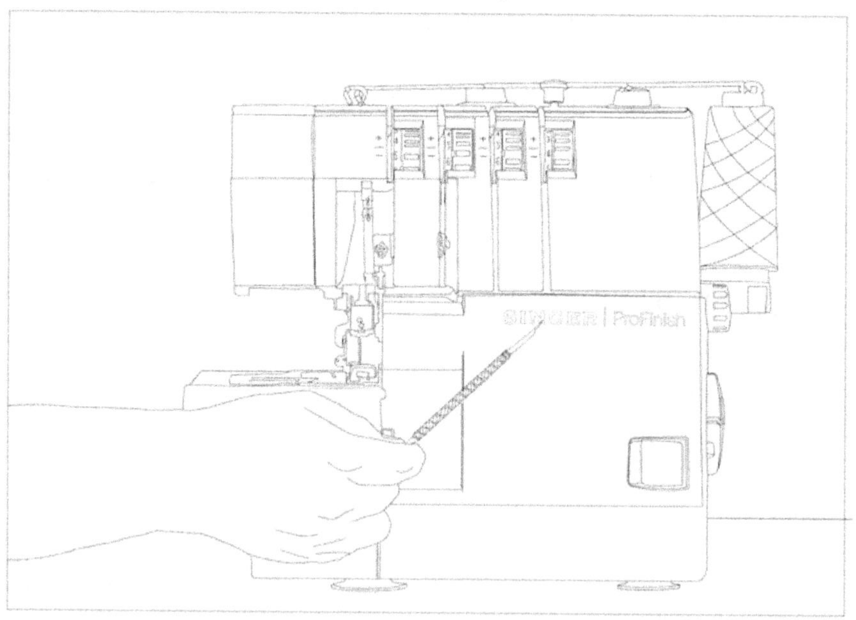

The basic serger machine is suitable for sewing simple fabrics of light to medium weight. You will not put your machine under pressure due to the use of heavy fabrics.

Features to look for:

3 and 4 thread stitches: It should have 3 to 4 threads ability to help you create desired stitches on the garment.

· Easy to thread: You should choose a machine with an easy to thread lower looper. Look for a machine that has a printed color-coded threading diagram.

Retractable knife: Whether the knife is retractable so that you can easily serge without cutting the edges of the fabric.

Differential feed: A good serging machine should have a differential feed to prevent your fabric from puckering or stretching out. Differential feed ensures you create a flat and smooth seam.

You can adjust the differential feed settings to have the front and the back feed dogs serge at different speeds.

Adjustable stitch length: Your basic serger machine should allow you to adjust stitch length and width.

Waste bin: A waste bin is an added advantage to your sewing room. Serging can be messy sometimes therefore, you need a waste bin to clear all fabric fibers mess created by your serger machine.

Free arm: I also recommend a serging machine with a free arm to sew tubes of fabric although you can still sew tubes without using the free arm. But if your machine has this feature, then it will save you a lot of time.

Most of the modern serger machines have features. However, some low-cost serger models do not have a waste bin or a free arm feature. So if you need to handle basic sewing projects, then this machine is suitable for you.

2. Experiment/Mid-range Serger machines

If you're the type of tailor who loves to experiment and create projects with different types of fabrics then you need to invest in a better-built serging machine.

Therefore, you need a serger that can sew 2, 3, and 4 thread stitches instead of just 3 and 4 stitching ability.

Features to look for:

All the features mentioned in the basic serger machine

2, 3, and 4 thread stitches: This will allow you to create different forms of stitches. For example, 2 thread mock flatlock stitch, 2 thread overlock stitches, and 2 thread rolled hemstitches.

Serger feet: Look for a serger that accommodates special presser feet and allows you to create more stitching effects. For example, a serger with gathering foot, buttonhole foot, ruffling foot, blind hem foot, etc.

Built quality: To enjoy the quality performance you need to look for a more durable machine with excellent motor power.

Rolled hem conversion: A good serger should make it easy to switch from normal overlocking stitches to rolled hemstitches.

Adjustable pressure: The best serger machine should allow you to easily adjust tension dials with numbers or markings and not through the use of screws.

High presser foot lift: Another factor you need to consider is the level of the presser foot lift. If you're serging thick fabrics, your serger should be able to support 5 to 6mm of the thickness or even allow 4mm fabric to fit underneath the foot.

3. Automatic/ Premium Serger machine

If you picked option 3, you're looking for a serger machine that is easy to use. This type of serger will automatically choose the tension dials for you. Just a push of a button and the serger will do the rest by itself.

These types of sergers are the most expensive in the market and worth the value for your money

Features to look for:

Includes all the features in basic and experiment serger machines

Looper air threading: The automatic serger should be able to thread fiddly looper by just pushing a button.

Automatic tension: With automatic tension, you don't have to figure what is the right tension settings for the fabric. The Serger will automatically select the right tension setting for you.

Built-in needle threader: If you have eyesight issues this feature will be of great help to you. It will thread the needles for you. No more wasting time trying to thread with your unsteady hands.

Built-in spreader/ 2 thread converter: This makes it easy to switch to 2 thread stitches and serge more quickly.

Other features to consider

1. How often do you sew?

If you're always using your machine every day then you should go for a machine that is more durable. The build quality of your machine will determine the performance and lifetime of your machine.

Cheap sergers are made from weaker metals, and weaker motors so they will have less power. They also have more plastic inside and other poor quality materials. Buying these types of sergers will compromise the machine performance and it will not last long.

If you sew daily, then premium and mid-range sergers are more suitable for you. But if you only sew occasionally, then you can go for the budget serger machines.

2. Do you use thick fabrics like canvas and denim to sew?

If your answer is yes, then you should buy a serger with;

Adjustable pressure: The serger should have user-friendly dials to allow you to easily adjust the tension dials. Modern serger machines have adjustable pressure that allows you to create more pressure when sewing thick fabric or reduce pressure when handling light fabrics.

Older sergers come with unmarked screws for you to change the pressure. And this can be difficult for you since the screws are unmarked compared to when adjusting pressure by a simple numbered dial.

Motor power: Buy a built-in machine with more motor power to give you better results. If you're serging thick fabrics they put more pressure on your machine. Therefore, you need a serger with more power and strong built-in quality to be able to handle the pressure.

High presser foot lift: You can go for sergers with a presser foot lift of about 5mm or 6mm. A 4mm lift is also high enough and can support up to 8 layers of medium-weight denim fabric underneath.

3. Do you have eyesight problems?

Those who have issues with their eyesight find it difficult to thread the needles and the loopers. In such cases then you need to buy a serger that has:

Built-in needle threader: This tool will automatically insert thread on the needles.

Air-threaded looper: By just pushing a button, you can automatically thread the loopers. This feature is mostly found in premium serger machines. It uses a compressor air to insert the thread inside the looper hole.

5 Best serger machines for Beginners

The review on these four types of serger machines is based on the delivered quality, ease of threading, quality of construction and price.

<u>1. Brother M343D Overlock Nachine</u>

The brother range serger is a budget-friendly machine and one of the best in the market. It has a great threading system and comes with several free accessories such as a waste tray, free arm, and an extension table.

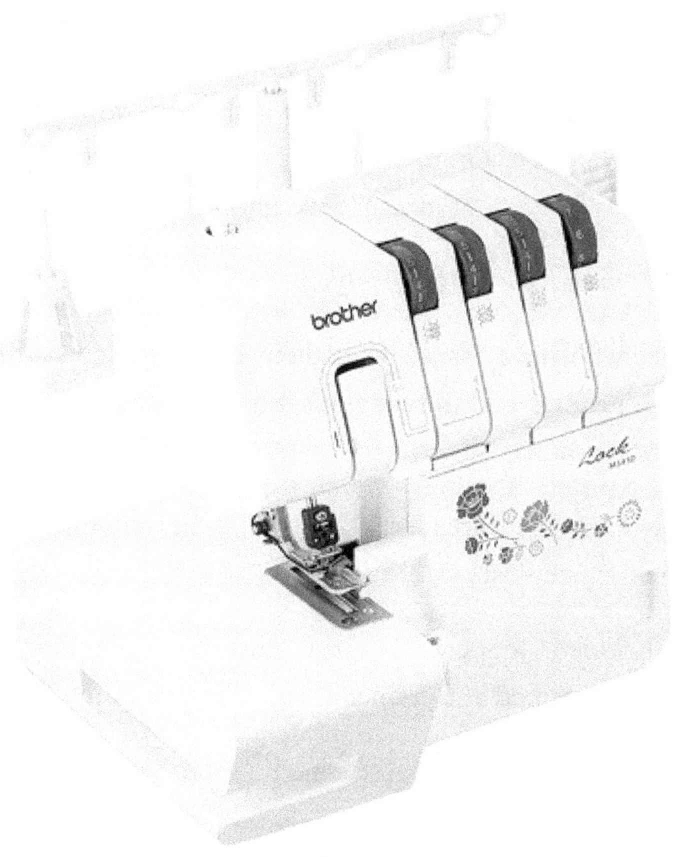

Image source: Amazon

This type of overlock is great for someone who sews occasionally.

With this budget overlock machine, you can only sew 3 or 4 thread stitches which is what most people use. If you're looking forward to doing 2 thread stitches, then you need to go for premium overlocks. It also uses the F.A.S.T lower looper threading system.

You can sew rolled hem, blind hem stitches, narrow hem, and mock flatlock with this type of overlock.

<u>2. Janome 6234XL Overlock</u>

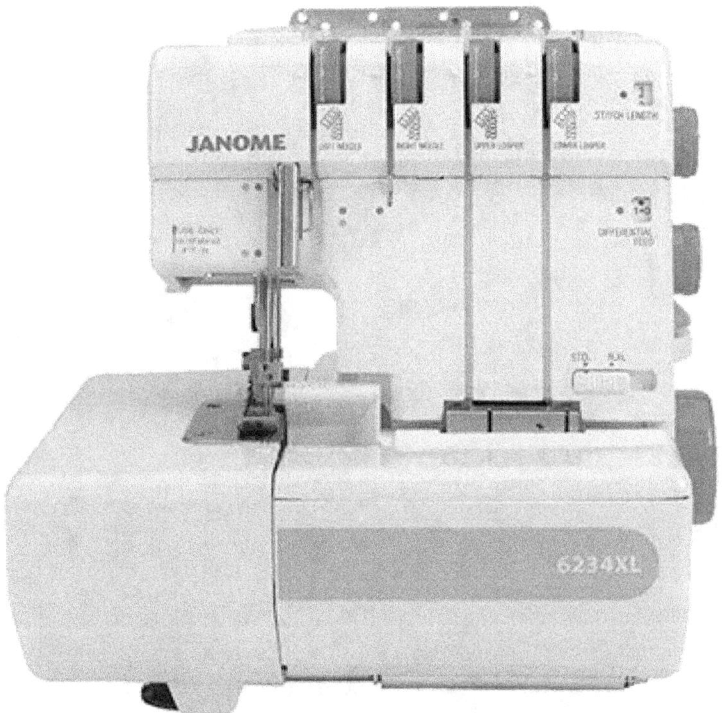

Image source: Amazon

This is great for creating professional looking stitches such as blind hem stitches, rolled hem, narrow, hem, and mock flatlock. You don't have to rely on 3 or 4 thread stitches, thanks to its 2 thread stitching ability.

This type of overlock has a better build quality that features a differential feed and a lower looper pre-tension setting slider. The color-coded thread guide makes your sewing much better.

Janome 6234XL is my overall best overlock machine for beginners.

3. Brother 2340CV

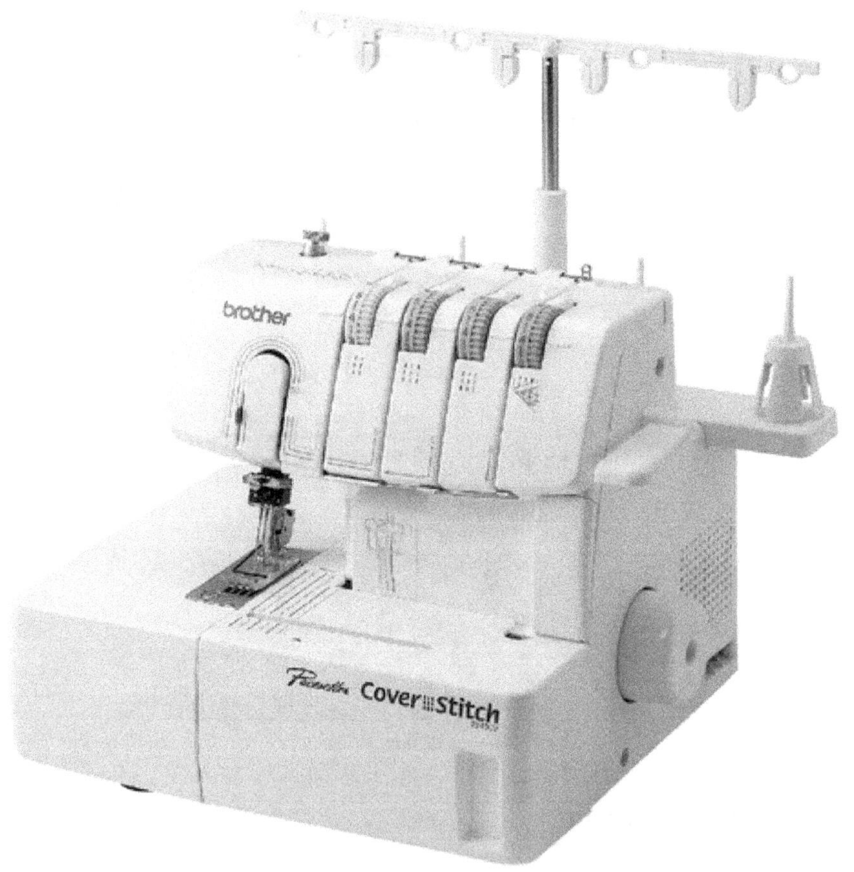

Image source: Amazon

Brother 2340CV is an easy to use overlock machine that supports 2, 3 and 4 stitch functions and adjustable stitch length. It features a tri-cover stitch with both wide and narrow cover stitches with easy to set color-coded threading.

You can easily adjust stitch length using a convenient dial. Test several stitch lengths to find the right stitch length for your project. A blind stitch foot is also included.

<u>4. Juki MO-2000QVP</u>

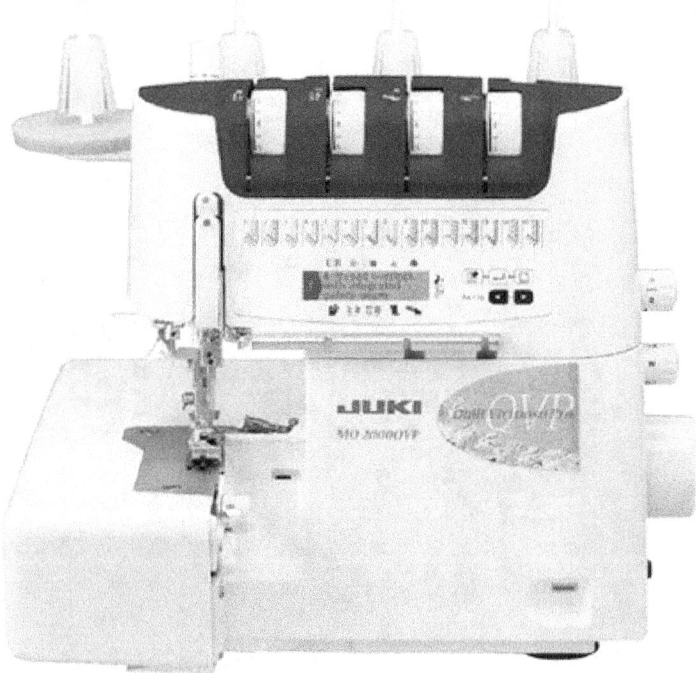

Image source: Amazon

This is great for those looking for an easy overlock machine that threads itself. It is among the best with an air threading technique and a needle threader. The machine will thread everything for you, you don't have to worry on how to thread your machine.

It has quality metal parts, high motor power, and other unique features. The lower looper converter can allow 2-3 thread conversion as well as do automatic rolled hemming. You can set up to 15 different stitches using this overlock.

Also, the overlock has an adjustable presser foot pressure and a wider throat area. An alternative to this is the Janome AT 2000D overlock or Juki MO-1000.

<u>5. Baby Lock Enlighten</u>

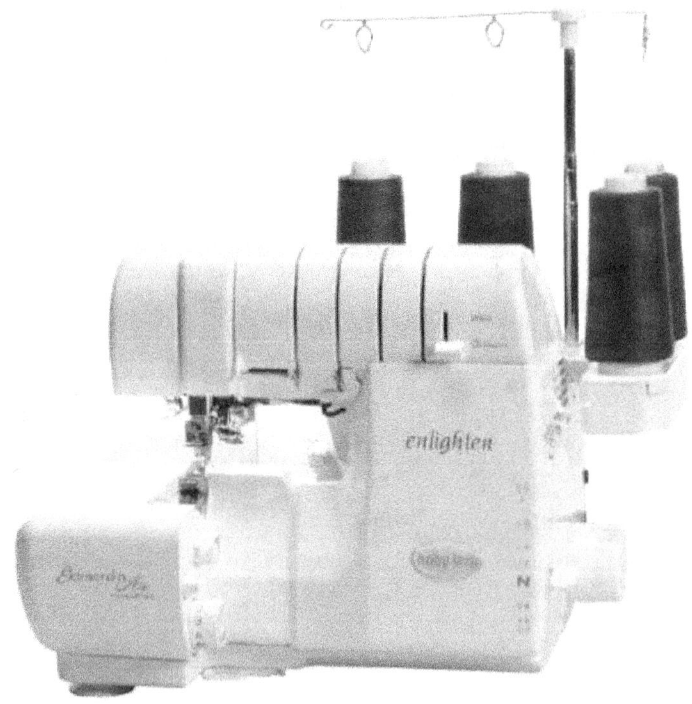

Image source: Amazon

This is an automatic air threading and automatic tension adjustment. It uses extraordinaire threading system to quickly thread your system and make life easy. It chooses your stitch settings automatically making it your dream machine.

Babylock has an excellent market reputation so you're assured of a quality product and it is worth the price.

If you're looking forward to the easiest overlock machine, then you will love this model.

Chapter Summary

There are a lot of serging tools in the market but the above-mentioned tools should be part of your top list in your serger accessories toolbox. The tools help you get started sewing using your serger machine.

Since you know the use of each of the tools, you can add them to your shopping list the next time you're walking to your local sewing accessory store. make sure you buy the best tools for your serger brand.

In the next chapter, you will learn how to thread a serger

CHAPTER THREE

How To Thread A Serger Machine

Do you dread threading your serger machine? Well, you're not alone. Many people have frustrating moments when it comes to changing threads in the machine.

You always have to open the overlock lid then ensure the thread passes through the right place and threaded correctly. Otherwise, your machine will not stitch.

In this chapter, you will learn step by step procedure on how to thread your serging machine and how to adjust your tension and stitches.

Tip: You must follow the threading order. In most machines, the order is the same but sometimes it can vary from one machine to the next. You should confirm the threading order from your serger manual before proceeding. Most machines follow Upper looper, lower looper, and needles order.

Let's get started!

Before you get started, make sure you have these basic tools for your 4-thread overlock machine   .

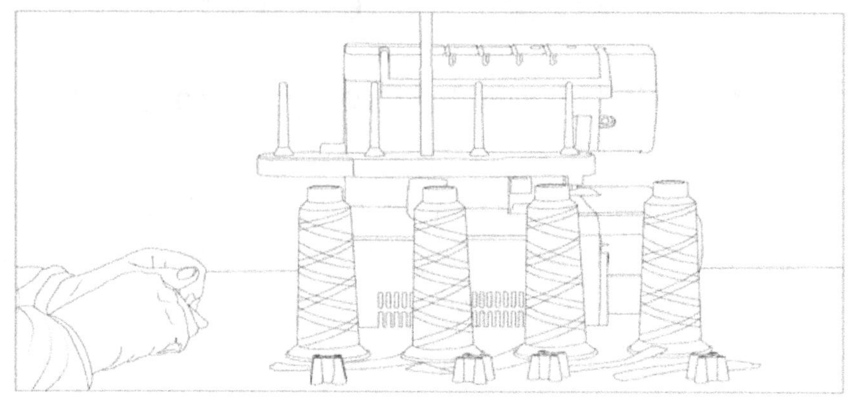

They include:

Overlock/Serger machine (In this case we will use Brother 1034D)

4 spools of thread (Preferably a cone thread because it's not easy to get snagged in the small thread clip as the regular thread spools do)

Tweezers

Small thread scissors or thread snips

Scrap fabric

Overlock manual

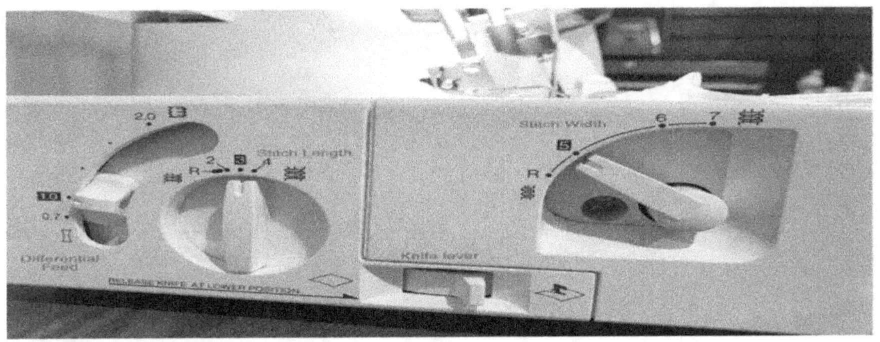

Before you start threading, always have a look at the settings of your overlock machine.

Stitch length: This determines how long your stitches should be. Based on your machine, you can choose your preferable stitch length. In this case, the numbers are in millimeters so I will choose 3mm.

Stitch width: This determines how thick or deep your stitches should be. They range from 5-7mm. You can choose a standard 5mm width since we are not doing any special hem.

Differential feed: It is used to control front and rear feed dogs' movements. That is, how will the feed pull the fabrics through? Set this to 1 so that the fabric is pulled evenly by both the front and rear feed dogs.

Knife/Blade lever: You can keep the blade down if you want to cut excess fabric while sewing.

Tension dials Setting: You can start by adjusting the tension to 4. This will make it easier when you want to adjust the stitch tension.

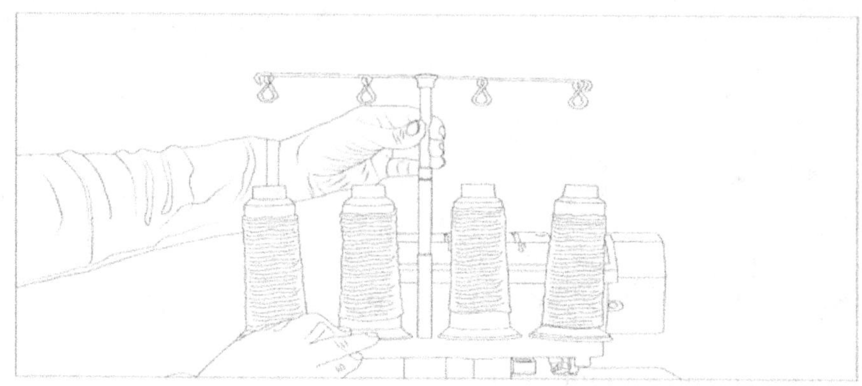

Threading a 4-thread Serger Machine

To practice with, you can use 4 different thread colors. You can choose colors similar to the tension dial colors. This will help you to know which dial you need to adjust later.

Place the 4 cone thread spools on each of the spool pins and extend the thread tree   .

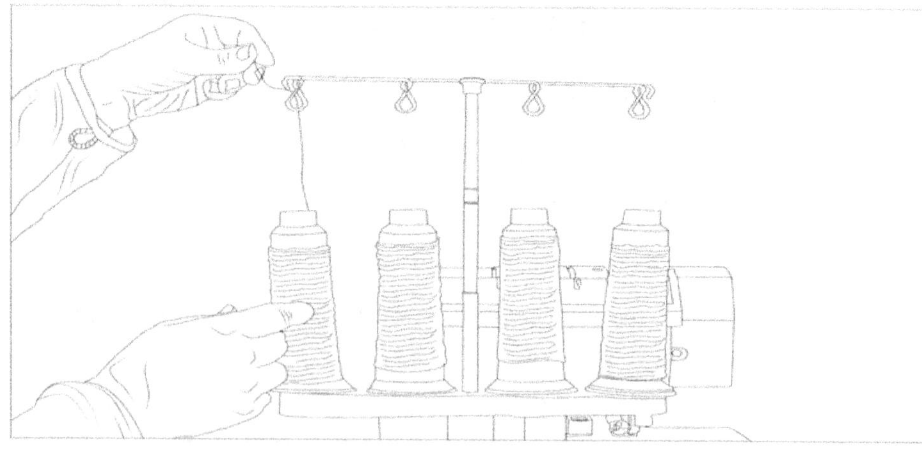

Each individual machine comes with an instruction manual on how to thread it. Your machine may have a slight difference from this one. Always consult your instruction manual for accurate threading.

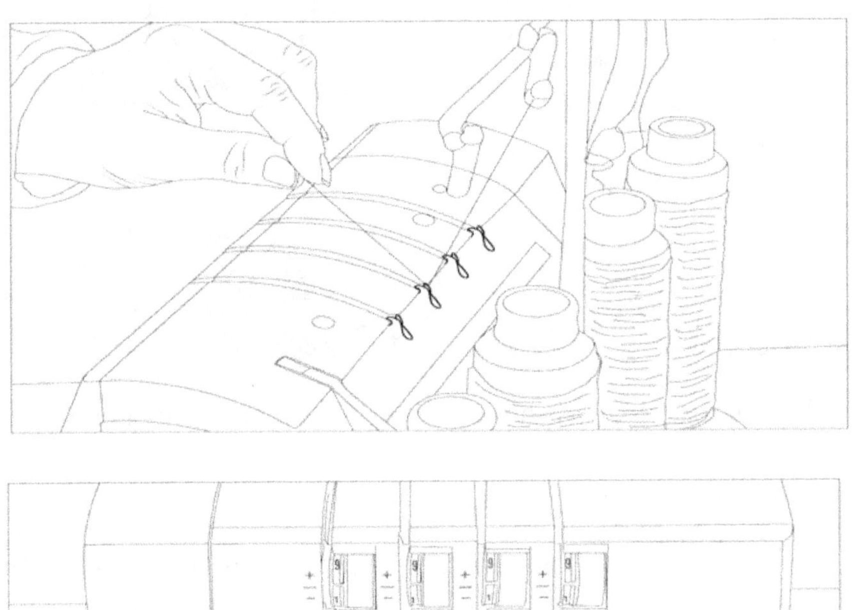

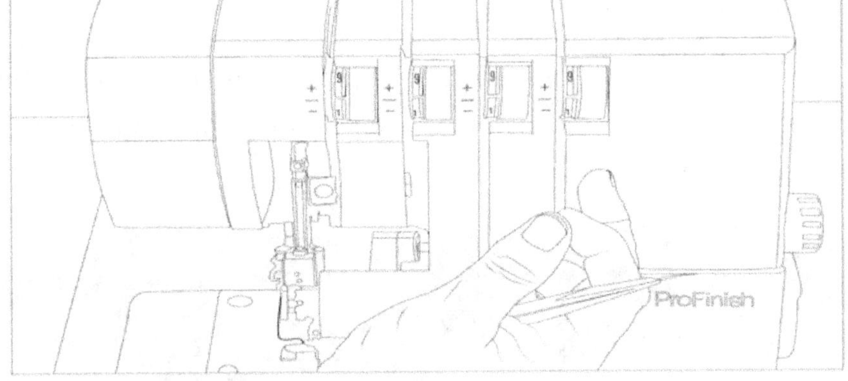

Steps to follow;

Threading the left needle

Step 1:

To thread the left needle, we will use the yellow thread color.

Pull the thread from the thread tree and pass it through the first guide hole on top of the machine as shown below.

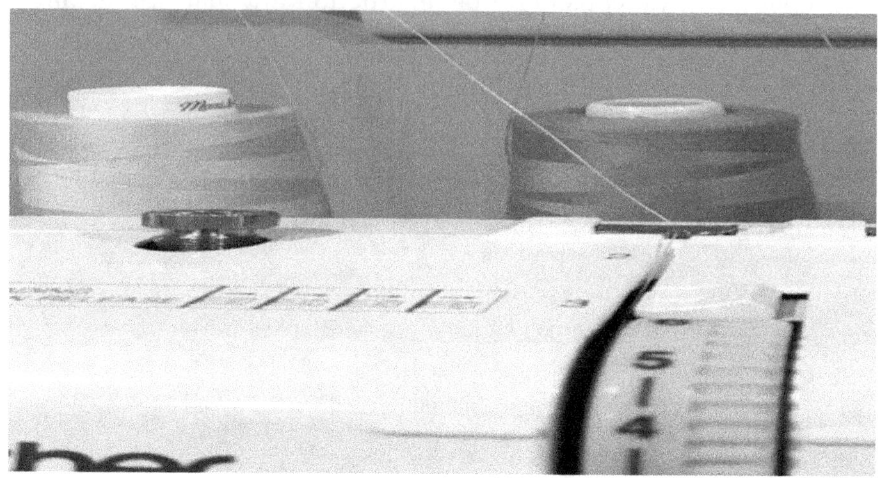

If your machine has some markings, you can follow them.

Step 2:

Pull the thread to pass through the tension disc (next to the first tension dial). Follow the instructions on your machine and get ready to thread the needle.

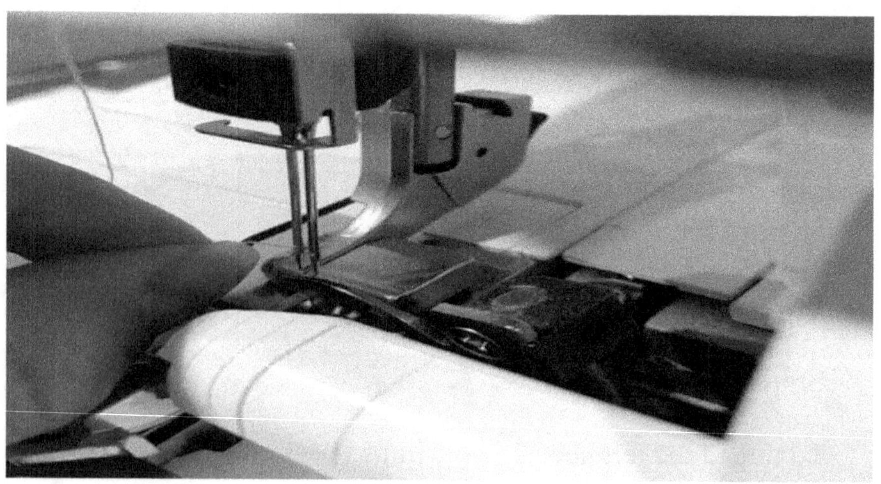

Step 3:

Thread your needle by passing the thread from front to back. You can use tweezers or use a needle threader to quickly thread your needles.

Step 4:

After inserting the thread, you can use tweezers to pull the thread to the back of the machine.

Threading the right needle

Step 1:

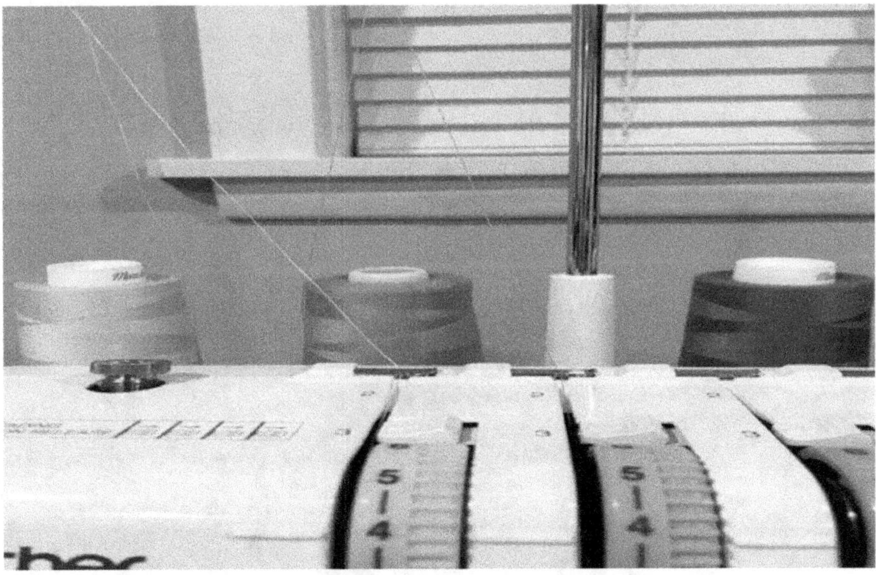

Pick your pink thread and pass it through the 2nd guide hole in the thread tree. Pass the thread through 2nd guide on the top of the machine as shown above. If your machine has markings always follow them.

Step 2:

Pull the thread to pass through the 2nd tension disc next to the tension dial. Pull the thread up and around the channel just like you threaded the left needle.

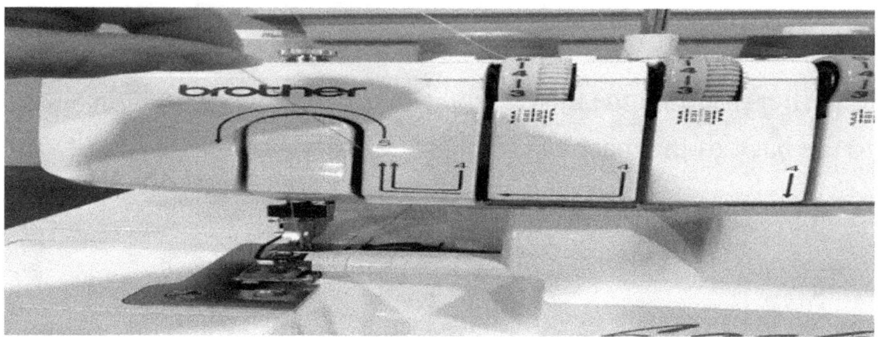

Step 3:

Insert the thread in the right needle from front to the back direction and push the thread to the back. You can also use tweezers to pull the thread.

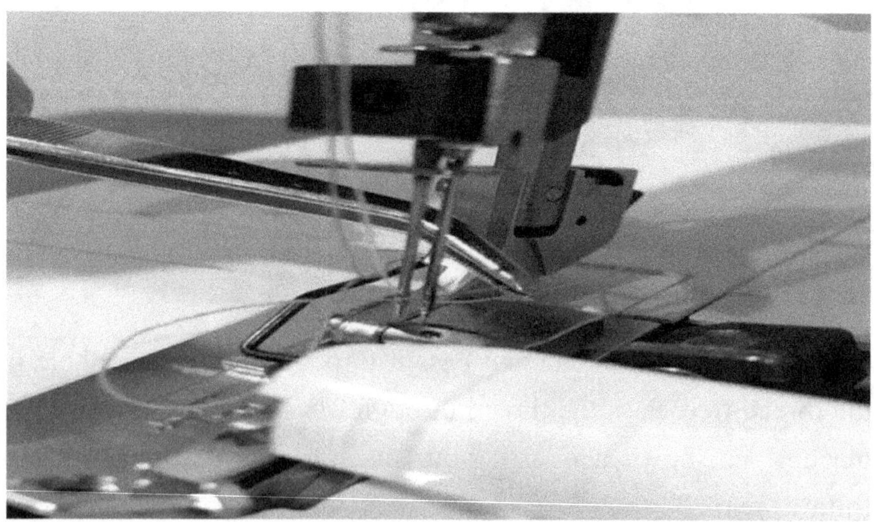

Now both threads (yellow and pink) should be lined up at the back of the machine.

Threading the upper looper

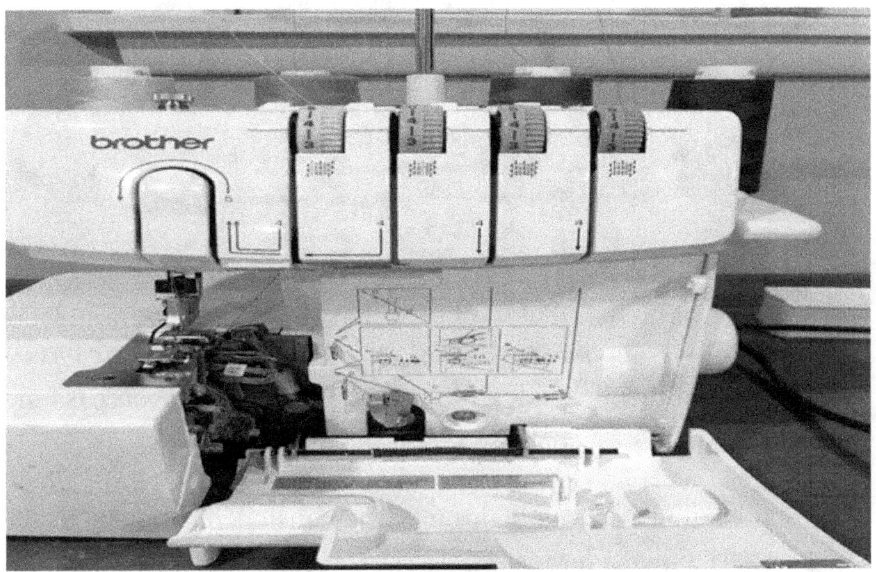

Start by pulling out the trim trap, you can slightly lift up the machine to make it easy to pull the trim trap and pull the front cover. This will enable you to access both lower and upper looper.

After pulling the front cover, there is a diagram that guides you on how to thread the upper and the lower loopers. Some machines might have a slightly different diagram so make sure to follow your machines diagram for you to thread correctly.

Step 1:

Using our third thread (green color), we can now thread the upper looper or the third needle.

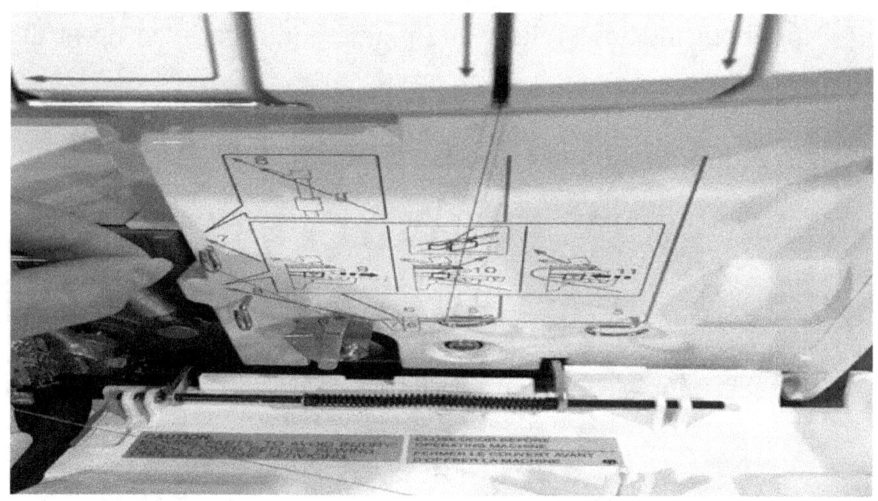

Just like threading the left and right needles, the third thread passes through the 3rd guide hole on the thread tree. Then pass the thread through the 3rd guide on top of the machine.

Pull the thread to pass through the tension disc (next to 3rd tension dial). Pull the thread through guides indicated by the diagram on the front cover.

Step 2:

Once you pass the thread through the indicated guide, you can now thread the upper looper needle. You can use tweezers to pull the thread front to the back.

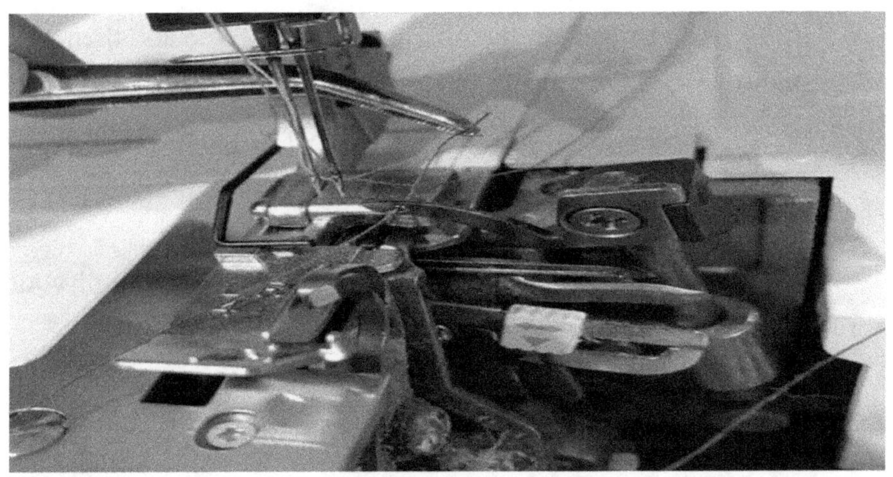

Pull the threat to the back of the machine as you have done with other threads.

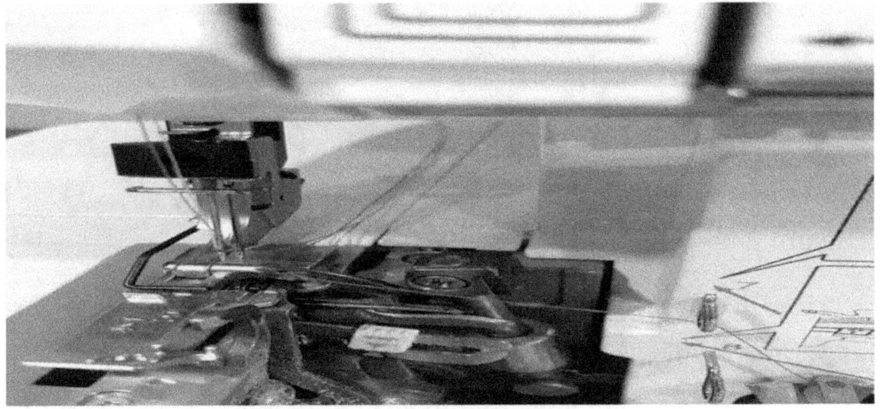

Threading the lower looper

We are going to use our 4th thread (blue color) to thread the lower looper.

Step 1:

Pass the blue thread via the hole in the thread tree and then pull it through the 4th guide at the top of the machine. Pass the thread through the 4th tension disc next to the last tension dial.

Step 2:

Follow the marked instructions on your machine and pull your thread through a series of steps on the front cover.

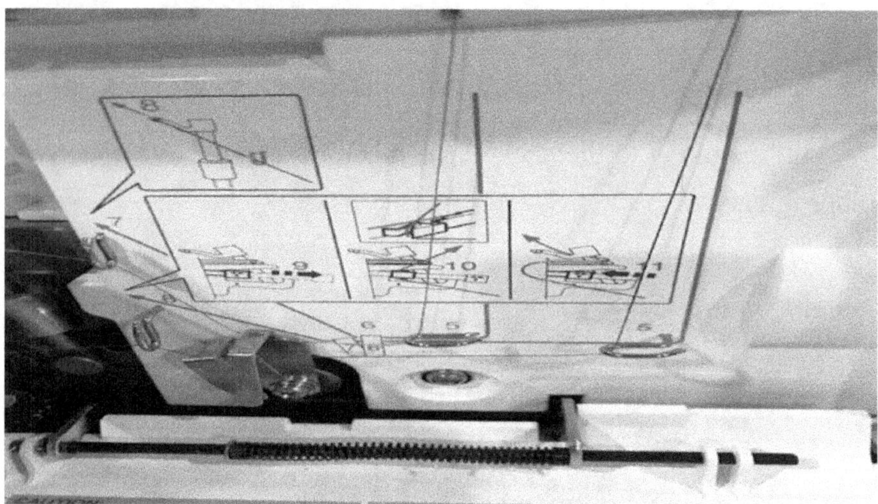

Now thread the lower looper with your thread. Thread on the two holes on your lower looper needle. Some machines do have an auto thread guide that automatically threads the first needle hole. Follow your machine instruction manual to know how the lower looper needle needs to be threaded.

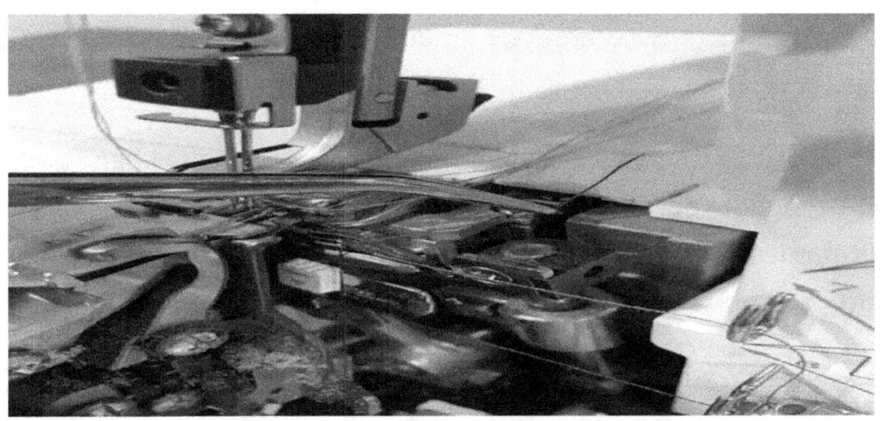

Step 3:

After threading, use tweezers to pull the thread to the back. The lower looper thread should always be placed at the top of the upper looper thread.

Step 4:

You can now close the front cover and return the trim tray back to its position. Line all 4 threads at the back of the machine before you start stitching.

Step 5:

Use the lever to lift up the presser foot of your serger machine and pass the 4 threads under the presser foot. Make sure the threads are pulled to the back. Now you're good to go!

Step 6:

Turn on your machine and step on the pedal. This will enable you to create a chain of threads. This also acts as a way of testing that the threads run through.

Since there is no breakage of any thread, you can now test the accuracy of your thread using the scrap fabric.

Place your fabric on the feed dogs to feed through. Align it with the edges of your machine and push the blade down. When the blade is pushed down, it will trim the excess fabric as you sew. The trimmed pieces will be collected in the trim trap.

When sewing, do not pull or push the fabric, let it feed through.

After stitching the scrap fabric, you can remove it from the machine and compare the tension.

Reviewing your overlock stitch and fixing issues

Once you make your first stitch on the scrap fabric, view the stitches formed at the front, back, and sides. Inspecting the stitches will confirm whether you have set the right tension dials based on the fabric type or whether there are issues that need to be fixed.

From our scrap fabric sample, if the blue thread (lower looper) at the front appears to be loose, this means you have to tighten the lower looper. This is done by adjusting the tension dial with the blue color thread.

Since the other colors look okay from the front view.

Proceeds to view the back of the fabric. If the yellow and pink color appear ok, then no adjustment needed on the tension dial. However, if the green and blue color thread appear loose, you need to tighten the tension dial with green and blue color (upper and lower looper tension) so that they can lay flat on the fabric edges.

Do the same for the side view of the fabric. Look at the overlock stitches on the sides where the two fabrics meet each other. If the settings are correct, you should see the loops perfectly lined down at the center. If any of the colors appear loose, you need to tighten it.

Having proper settings for the tension dials will leave your stitches looking professional.

How to change threads

Once you have already threaded your serger machines, it becomes easy to change the threads.

You don't have to open the lid in order to change the threads. You don't have to go through the threading process again. You can do that in just a few steps.

"How to change your serger thread and never re-thread again" is one of the best sewing hacks for every sewer. If you have been sewing for some time and you don't know this trick, it's time to learn it! And you will never be frustrated again while threading your machine. It will also save you time!

Step 1:

Turn off the machine and lift up the presser foot and ensure the needles are set at the highest point

Step 2:

Cut the thread close to the thread cone. Leave the piece of thread hanging and remove the thread.

Step 3: Your secret trick

Now put the cones of the new thread where you removed the old thread. Make sure the thread is placed in the right place.

Take the ends of the cut old thread and the new thread and tie a knot to them. Make sure the knot is strong and small. A simple knot is enough.

Step 4:

Pull the corresponding old thread color at the foot. Start by separating the 3 or 4 threads.

Step 5:

Pull the threads one by one until the new thread you have replaced is pulled to the back of the machine.

If the thread gets stuck along the way like in the tension disc, you can use your free hand to pull the thread. Continue pulling until the new thread comes up to the needle hole.

Due to the knot you made, the thread may not pass through the needle hole so you need to cut the knot then thread your needle again with the new color thread.

As simple as that, you're able to re-thread your machine. Repeat the same for all other threads you need to change and start sewing

Chapter Summary

Before you start your sewing projects you need to know how to thread your overlock machine. With the above steps, you will be able to correctly thread your needles and both upper and lower loopers. Incorrect threading may result in the breakage of thread.

After threading the needles, you can test them on your scrap fabric and adjust the tensions accordingly.

After the initial threading of your machine, changing the thread colors becomes easy and can be done in seconds. All you need is to cut the old thread around the thread tree and replace it with the new thread color. Take the edges of the cut old thread and the new thread edges and tie them together to create a knot. Then pull the replaced thread at the back of your machine until the new thread color reaches the needle hole, cut the knot, and thread the needle with the new color thread.

You can re-thread the other colors based on your preferences and you're good to start stitching.

In the next chapter, you will learn how to stitch overlock stitches.

CHAPTER FOUR

Introduction to Stitching Overlock Stitches

In our last chapter, we discussed how to set up your overlock machine and thread it. After threading your machine, now you're ready to start stitching. An overlock machine allows you to create a variety of stitches. A standard overlock machine should allow you to create at least 16 different forms of stitches.

Simple settings to your machine including adjusting the tension will help you create these different stitches. Your ability to customize the control settings is what makes the overlock machine great.

The most essential stitch to create is the overlock stitch. So whenever we talk of serging, most people only think of the overlock stitch but there are other different forms of stitches you can create with your overlock machine.

An overlock stitch is a special stitch that sews the edges of a piece of cloth by either adding hems, seams or edges.

You can sew an overlock stitch in different ways but the most used method is to sew a seam while at the same time finishing the raw edges of the fabric.

Overlock stitches are versatile since you can use them for decoration, construction, or for reinforcement of the fabric.

These stitches are created when one of the needles (or two needles) penetrates through the fabric to sew a seam and the knife blade trims the edges of the fabric while the looper thread wraps the clean raw edge of the fabric.

A stitch can be formed using different ways based on the number of threads used. The key factor is the durability of your stitches.

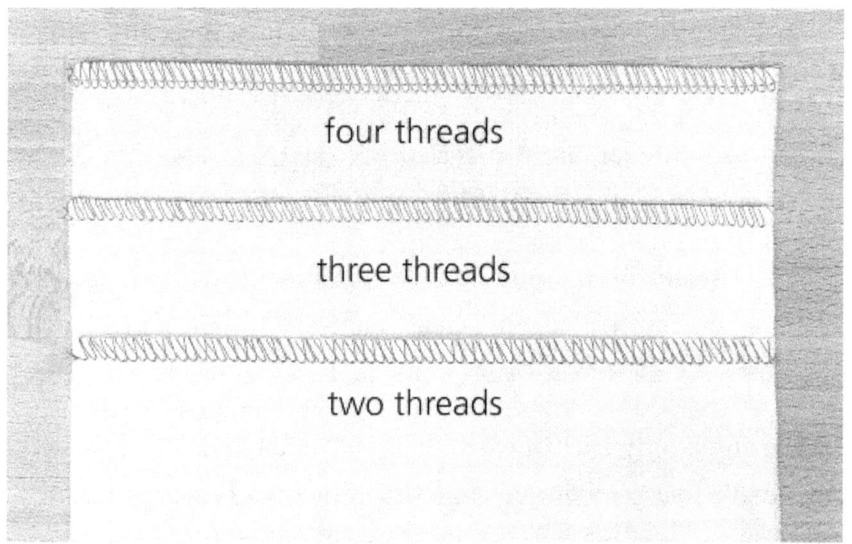

Types of overlock stitches

There are different types of overlock stitches that are classified based on the number of threads used in making the stitch. Most overlock machines use 1, 2, 3, 4, and 5 thread formations.

Each of these threads serves a unique purpose and benefits. For example;

1 - Thread: It is great for doing end-to-end seams or butt-seaming on a piece of garment finishing.

2 – Thread: Great for edging and seaming on knits and woven. You can use this type of stitch to finish seam edges, stitch an elastic lace to lingerie, stitch flatlock seams, and hem.

In 2-thread stitch, the needle thread appears at the bottom of the fabric while the looper threads are on top of the fabric. Both needle and looper threads intersect at the edges of the fabric.

This thread is suitable for sewing lightweight and stretchy fabrics.

2-thread stitches are are not strong enough to create a seam, they're only suitable for finishing the raw edges of your fabric.

3 – Thread: It is used to sew pintucks, blind hems, create finishing on fabric edges, create narrow rolled hems, create decorative edging, create seam knits, and woven fabrics.

The stitch only uses one needle, you can choose either the left or right needle to create simple edge finishing on lightweight fabrics. It is the most used stitch due to its wide application. If you want to sew a loose t-shirt, you can use this type of stitch.

4 – Thread: Used to create decorative edges and finishing, seam high-stress areas, and to create mock safety stitches that add extra strength on the stitches while at the same time retaining flexibility.

The 4-thread overlock stitch uses two needle threads to sew two rows of stitches in fabric while the looper thread wraps the edges of the fabric. The stitch is suitable for sewing medium to heavyweight fabrics, or sewing seams in fitted garments.

A 4-thread overlock allows you to sew more flexible seams and the stitches are more durable. Since more threads are used, you may end up with a bulky seam especially if you use thicker threads.

5 – Thread: Mostly used in apparel manufacturing. They utilize the use of two needles to create a very strong seam.

Stitch formation

1. As the needle goes through the fabric, a loop of thread is formed at the back of the needle.

2. As the needle moves downward into the fabric, the lower looper moves from left to right. The tip of the lower looper needle passes behind the needle via the loop of thread that has already been formed behind the needle.

3. The lower looper continues to move towards the right side. As it moves forward, the lower thread is carried along via the needle thread.

4. When the lower looper moves from left to right, the upper looper moves from right to the left. The upper looper tip goes behind the lower looper needle and picks the lower looper thread and thread the needle.

5. After needle threading, the lower looper moves back to the far end of the left position. While the upper looper continues moving to the left it firmly holds both the lower looper thread and the needle thread in place.

6. 6.   The needle will again begin its downward move and pass behind the upper looper to promptly secure the upper

looper thread. The needle will pass between metal and thread. This will result in a complete overlock stitch formation. This process continues until you finish sewing the fabric   .

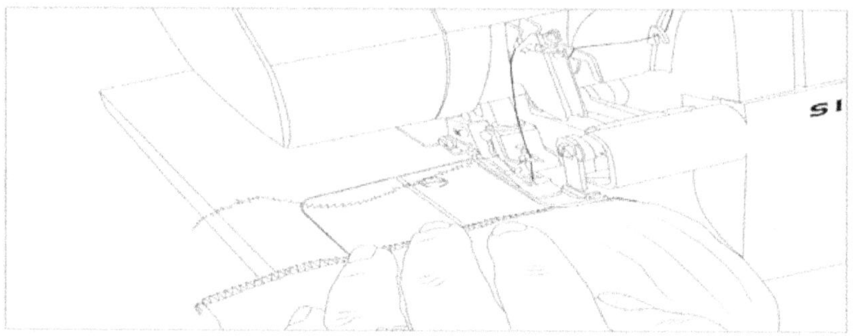

When to use an overlock stitch

Overlock stitch is ideal for sewing garments and creating general edge finishing regardless of the number of threads you use. You can use the stitch to construct a complete garment and finish the edges at the same time.

Overlock stitches help you join two pieces of fabric together. Some fabrics require you to create overlock raw edges before you can sew them. For example, the fabrics that need to be pressed open after you have sewn on them in order to reduce the fabric bulkiness. In such cases, you have to overlock the raw edges, then you can later construct your garment.

If your garment needs to be fitted with patterns that require extra attention, then you have to construct the patterns to the garment and then later you can add finishing edges with your overlock machine.

Therefore, based on what you want to sew, there are cases where you sew the garment and at the same time create finishing edges. While there are cases where you have to start sewing the fabric and later add the finishing edges. Alternatively, start with finishing edges then sew your garment.

Creating a Perfect overlock stitch

Since overlock stitch is the default stitch in all serger machines regardless of the number of threads used, the default stitch settings are always indicated on the machine using a small dot. These dots are on the tension dials next to number 4   .

	Stitch Type	Needle Positions	Tension Dial: Numbers shown are average settings on medium weight fabric with standard #80 polyester spun thread					Page
			Blue	Green	Orange	Yellow	Upper Looper or Spreader	
1	Two-Threaded Wrapped Edge Overlock (502)	3.5mm		3.0		1.5	Spreader	30
		5.7mm	3.0			1.0	Spreader	
2	Two-Threaded Standard Rolled Hem Stitching (503)	3.5mm		0.5		6.0	Spreader	31
		5.7mm	0.5			6.0	Spreader	
3	Three-Threaded OverLock (504)	3.5mm		3.0	2.5	2.0	Upper Looper	32
		5.7mm	2.5		2.5	2.0	Upper Looper	
4	Three-Threaded FlatLock (505)	3.5mm		0.5	5.5	5.5	Upper Looper	33
		5.7mm	0.5		5.0	6.0	Upper Looper	
5	Three-Threaded Wrapped Edge Overlock	3.5mm		3.0	0.5	7.0	Upper Looper	34
		5.7mm	3.0		0.5	7.0	Upper Looper	
6	Four-Threaded Ultra Stretch Mock Safety Stitch (514)		2.5	2.0	2.5	2.0	Upper Looper	35

The same is applicable to the differential feed, stitch length, and also the cutting width, If you have all the settings adjusted to the recommended numbers, then you have a solid overlock stitch.

But depending on the fabric you want to be sewn and the type of thread, the default settings may not work for you.

Probably if you're a beginner, you may not know whether you have the perfect stitch for your fabric. But as you continue to learn to use the machine, you can fine-tune the stitches. I suggest you follow the above steps mentioned in our previous chapter to fine-tune the stitches. That is, thread the machine with colored threads that match the marked or labeled path of your machine.

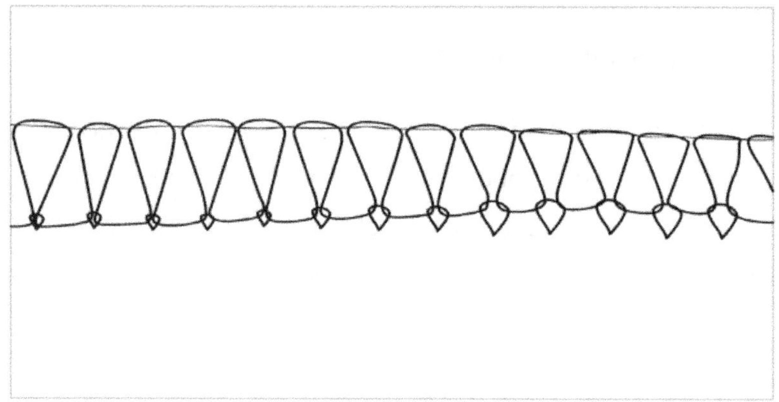

With different colors, you can identify the loose color thread or a tight color thread and adjust the corresponding thread color tension dial accordingly.

The looper threads should always meet at the edge of the fabric so if there is an issue with the tension, you will notice that based on how they appear on the sewn fabric. If the upper looper thread is pulled to the back of the lower looper thread is pulled to the front, you need to adjust the tension and strike the balance on the two looper threads.

If you can see the looper threads on the front side where the needle penetrates the fabric, then you have a tight needle thread and you need to loosen the needle tension.

However, if the needle tension is too loose, you will not have clean and straight line stitches. This is because the looper thread will keep pulling the needle thread to the front and back of the seam allowance on the fabric.

Lastly, if the seam allowances are pulled too tight and the looper threads hang loosely on the edges of the fabric then you need to adjust your micro thread control (MTC). Micro thread control is a lever that is used to control the stitch finger.

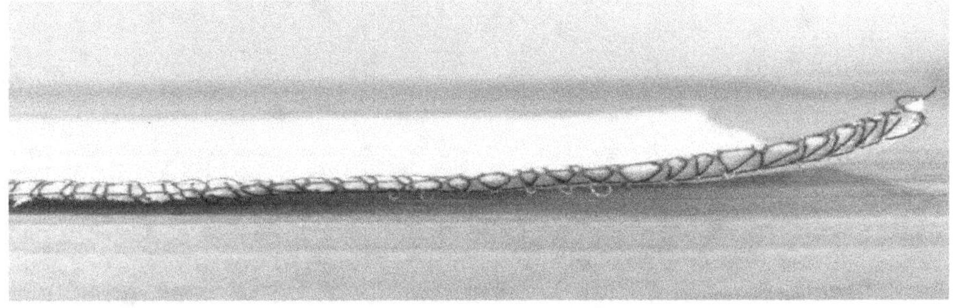

A stitch figure is a small metal around the needle area that supports the fabric as the loopers wrap the raw edges. If you increase the MTC (micro thread control) tension, the stitch finger will move out creating more space between the threads and the fabric. Reducing the tension will force the stitch finger to move in and bring the threads closer to the raw edges. This eliminates looping and results in tunneling of stitches.

If MTC is too tight, the looper thread digs into the raw edges of the fabric. This prevents the tunneling effect and the seam will not lie flat. If MTC is too loose, there will be slacks created between the looper threads and the edges of the fabric.

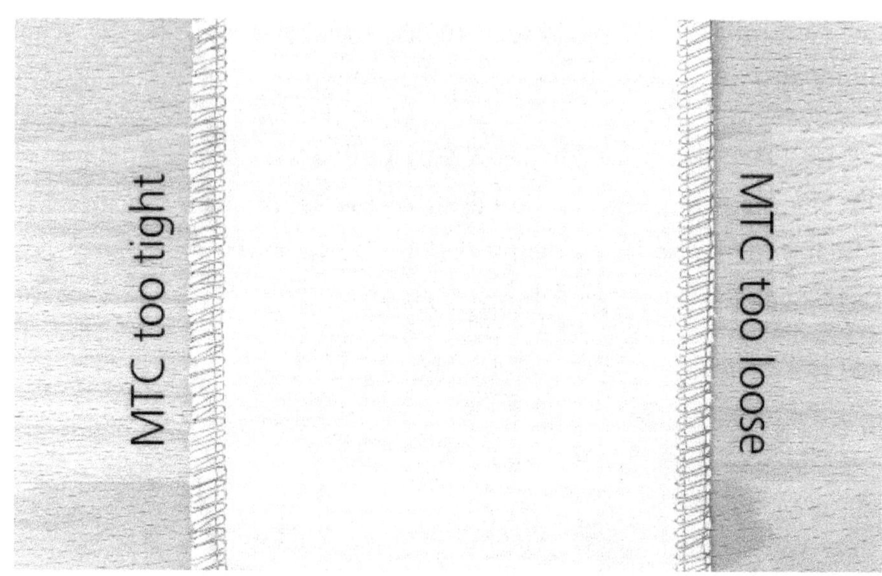

Therefore, to create a perfect stitch, you need to create a balance between the thread loopers and the needle threads.

Choosing the right serging stitches for your project

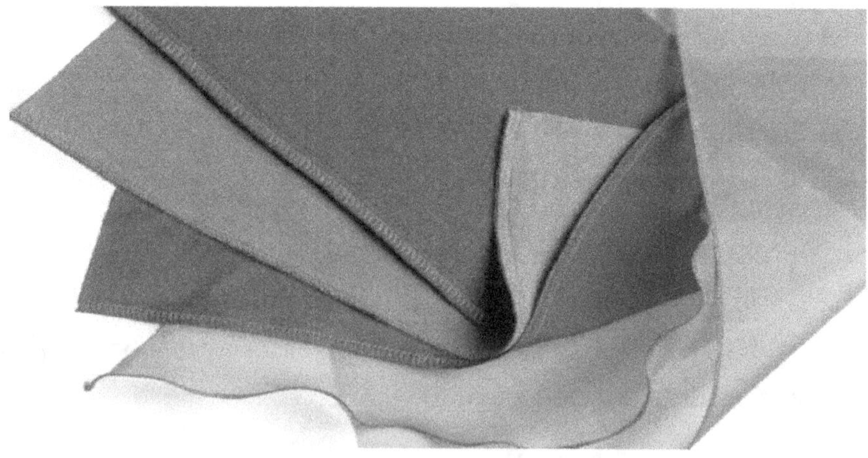

When serging, probably you have come across different stitches and you have been wondering what different stitches mean and how you can do them. Don't worry, you in the right place.

Overlock stitch, rolled hem and narrow hem are the most known stitches, but there are a variety of stitches you can form with your serger machine.

A serger stitch strengthens seams, add stretch to fabric, simplify edge finishing, and embellish your garment.

With the different types of stitches, sometimes you may be confused on which stitch to use and when. For you to choose the best stitch for your fabric, you need to first know the standard serger stitches.

Again, keep in mind that not all sergers that do all these stitches, so be sure to check with your brand on what type of stitches it can do. When buying a new serger, go for the one with the stitches you need.

The main stitches done by an overlock machine include:

· 3 and 4 thread overlock: It helps create seams and eliminate fraying of the fabrics raw edges.

· 2 thread overlock: It helps create lightweight stitches and also create finish stitches on lightweight fabrics.

· Wrapped stitches: In this, the lower looper thread wraps around the edges of the fabric from front to the back. You can use a 2-thread seam to create wrapped stitches that are strong and stretchy. You can use a decorative thread on the loopers to make the finish look good.

· Rolled hem and narrow hem: These types of stitches helps add finishing to a single layer of fabric. If your serging a sheer fabric, a rolled hem will add a beautiful finish to your garment. · In a rolled hem, the edges of the fabric are folded and then wrapped with threads. The hems are great for finishing edges on a silk scarf, chiffon dress, and edges of a ruffle.

You can use this stitch with lightweight fabrics to stop them from frying but it cannot be used for creating seams.

A narrow hem works the same as rolled hems but have a line that runs along the edges of the fabric. Narrow hems don't have full stitch look so you may have some gaps between the stitches. Therefore, if you're using a fabric that frays, then rolled hem will the most suitable stitch for your fabric.

· Flatlock: A flatlock helps you join two pieces of fabric side-by-side and create a flat seam. This type of seam is mostly found in sportswear garments because they need to be more comfy on the inside. When you sew wrong sides together, the lower looper thread remain outside the stitch but when you sew right side, the needle thread is placed outside.

This stitch is good for stretchy fabrics or when you want to sew a reversible stitch that look neat on both sides.

The flatlock only joins two pieces together without forming a seam allowance that rubs against your skin when exercising. If you want to join thick layers of fleece fabric, use this stitch to join them.

· Blind hem stitches: They are used to create invisible finish of the hems. You can use blind hems on your dresses and trousers made of woven fabric. You can also use bling hem in a stretchy t-shirt. Loosen the needle thread if you want the created hem to stretch with the fabric.

· Picot edge: This type of stitch is used to create decorative finish on the edges of a single layer of fabric. The serger folds the edges and wraps them with a thread

Therefore, when you want to create edge finishing or seams, choose the best stitch that will match your fabric needs.

One of the best stitch rules is to choose overlock stitches when handling standard seams on knits and wovens, a wider overlock stitch when dealing with bulky fabric, a narrow stitch with few threads when serging lightweight fabrics, and a wrapped stitch when knitting seams for maximum stretch.

If your machine can stitch 2-thread or 3-thread stitches, you can decide to use the left needle to sew wider stitches, or use the right needle for narrow stitches. Alternatively, you can decide to use rolled-hem stitches to create decorative narrow stitches. Since both loopers do not pierce through the fabric, you can decide to use a heavy or decorative thread in one or both of the loopers to make your edge finishing more attractive.

Chapter Summary

An overlock stitch is the most used stitch to join pieces of fabric together or add finishing to your garments. Creating this type of stitch is very easy, all you need is to learn how to customize your thread tension and you're good to go.

There are different types of stitches you can create like French seams, zigzag stitches, blind hems, and much more. For you to be able to create the different types of stitches using different thread types, you need to know how to create a perfect stitch for your projects.

Balancing the looper threads and needle threads can make it easy to sew a clean garment. The stitch ensures the edges of the fabric have a great finishing.

Also, if the stitches are far apart, then you will not have a strong seam especially if your serging on a loosely woven fabric. Therefore, you should adjust the thread tensions depending on the fabric you're using.

In the next chapter, you will learn how to stabilize your Serging stitches

CHAPTER FIVE

Stabilizing Serging Stitches

In our previous chapter, we have talked about how to balance your threads to have a perfect stitch. Based on the fabric you're using, you will find you have to adjust the tension dials for you to have a clean stitch.

Your fabric type affects how your stitches will turn out. If you're using a medium weight fabric, you may find adjusting the tension to a certain number will give you a good stitch. However, this stitch setting may not look good when used on thin or heavy fabric. The looper threads may appear either too loose or have a tight thread if used on heavyweight fabric.

So there are instances where adjusting the tension alone or even the presser foot may not balance your stitches. Therefore, implementing the stabilization of seams can help improve the quality and look of your stitches. Especially if you have a very thin fabric.

You may also want to reinforce the stitches in some of the high-stress areas or probably want to ensure your seams are sewn in a straight line and do not warp out of shape. Since overlock stitches do stretch as the fabric stretches, stabilizing the stitches will a great way to improve the stitches' look.

There are some great ways to stabilize your stitch such as using stay tape, using a ribbon, binding, or using a clear elastic.

These methods are great for stabilizing high-stress areas such as the shoulder seams.

In this chapter, you will learn how to stabilize your seams and reasons why you need to stabilize.

Stabilization of seams

Stabilizing helps prevent the fabric from stretching out. They act as a reinforcement to the seams especially if you're using knit fabric.

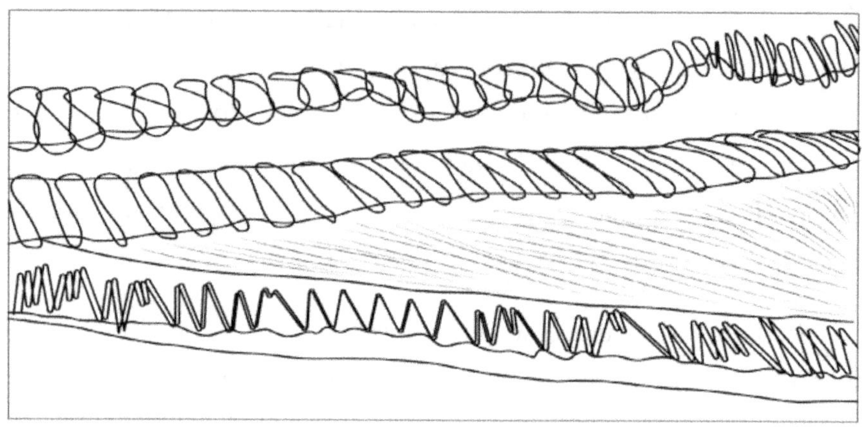

Most people always stabilize the shoulder seams because they are at high risk of stretching out when sewn and when you wear the garment.

The front piece of shoulder seam is sewn slanted thus, increasing the stretch of the garment. This makes you end up with a wider shoulder seam than your original pattern.

For this reason, you have to reinforce shoulder seams on t-shirts and on knit-tops.

There are various ways you can do this, but what is the best method for you to use? keep reading to learn how you can reinforce seams and when to use each of the methods mentioned.

Stabilizing methods

Clear elastic

Power fusible

Fabric strip

Fusible bias tape

1. Clear elastic

This is the most common stabilizing method because it has the ability to stretch and recover just like the 4-way stretch of spandex knits. Therefore, clear elastic has a perfect stretch for almost all the fabrics and makes your fabric stay in shape.

Clear elastic is suitable for sewing any close-fitting stretchy tops. It ensures you don't end up with an uneven shoulder seam.

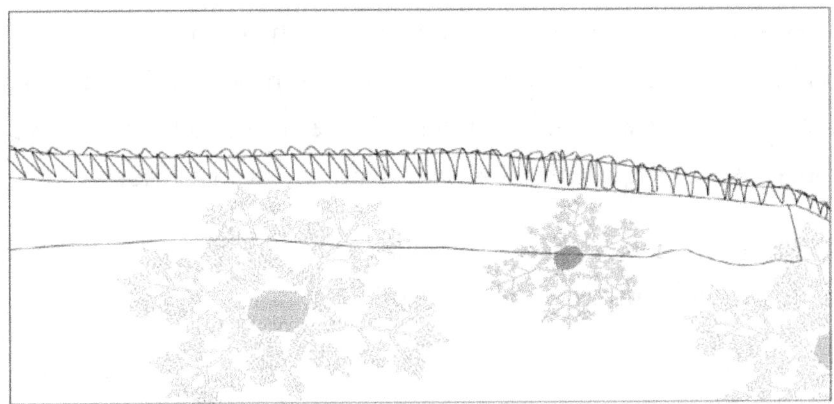

The width of this clear elastic is equivalent to your seam overlock stitch, so you can use the clear elastic to cover your shoulder seam.

No need to fuse the clear elastic thus making it suitable for use with synthetic knits. It is also easy to serge clear elastic especially if your presser foot has a built-in narrow elastic slot.

However, the clear elastic doesn't work well if you're sewing a neckline using an attachment binder because you have to open the shoulder seam making it difficult to add the clear elastic later. Again, not all people who like to have the silicon feel of the clear elastic on their clothing. Also, the clear elastic learning curve can frustrate you.

You should always sew the clear elastic together with shoulder seams at the same time and only cut the elastic after you have sewn both seams.

You can also use clear elastic when gathering the fabric in order to add some shirring to your garment.

2. Power Net/Power Fusible

Power net is a piece of a heavy stretch mesh that is used to reinforce stability on lingerie and shapewear products. Just like clear elastic, the power net has a good balance for stretch and recovery properties making it great for sewing stretchy knit fabrics.

You don't need to fuse it and due to his versatile nature, you can use this stretchy mesh on any type of fabric.

3. Fabric strip/Ribbon

This one of the greatest methods that relies on the use of fabric scraps and it the most commonly used method in the garment industry. Scraps made from 100% cotton jersey or a blend of cotton and jersey are the best in stabilizing shoulder seams.

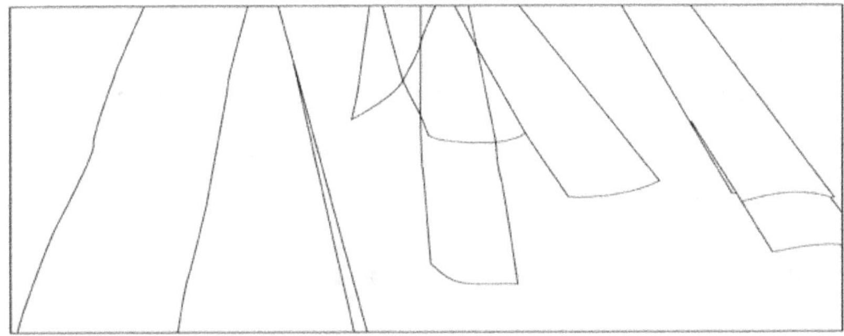

Make sure to use a thin knit with a smidgen stretch length to reinforce seams. Cut the strips vertically and use them to sew the seams. The fabric strip adds stability to your garment and also gives your knits the right amount of stretch.

A fabric strip is versatile and can be used in reinforcing almost any type of fabric. Although, when used on shoulder seams, it can add some bulkiness to them.

When stabilizing shoulder seams and knits, place the reinforcement strip on the back shoulder piece and sew the seam.

You can also attach the fabric strip to your garments by using either glue or zigzag stitch and then go ahead and sew the shoulder seam. This ensures the strip doesn't slip while sewing the seam.

4. Fusible bias tape

A fusible tape is great for adding a balance between the stability of the garment and its stretch. Make sure to use the bias tape to get better results. It is easy to sew since you only stuck the tape on the fabric and sew the shoulder seam.

The tape doesn't fuse well when sewing synthetic fibers.

Alternatively, you can use stay tape or cotton twill tape which is soft and made of natural fiber. These tapes prevent stretching of seams since the tapes themselves do not stretch

How to stabilize the shoulder seam

Prepare a piece of your stabilizer. You can cut it to about 1 to 2 inches longer than the seam.

Place the two pieces of the bodice together with the wrong sides facing together.

Place the aligned pieces of fabric under the presser foot.

Place the stabilizer fabric on top of the bodice pieces at an exact place intended for the seam line and the excess length remains under the presser foot.

Serge at the middle of the stabilizer up to the end of the seam

Trim the excess stabilizer on both ends of the seam.

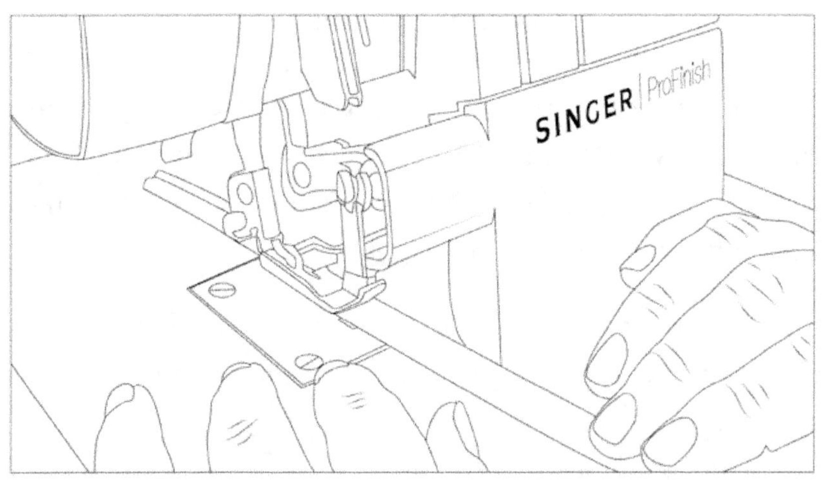

SINGER | ProFinish

Chapter Summary

Stabilization of seams is one of the greatest methods you can use to strengthen your seams, especially when dealing with stretchy fabrics or lightweight fabrics. They make it to reinforce stitches when dealing with a very thin or light fabric.

It also helps prevent fabrics from stretching out. Some stabilizing methods enhance the design of the garment by hiding the seam allowance.

You can use binding strips, clear elastic, twill/stay tape to stabilize your seams. Depending on the material you're using, you can use any of the stabilizing methods to strengthen your seams.

In the next chapter, you will learn how to add corner curves both inside and outside and circle curves.

CHAPTER SIX

Working With Corner and Curves

A serger machine makes the finishing of your fabric look clean and more professional. However, serging finishing edges around the corners and curves can be difficult not only to beginners but also to those who have been sewing for some time.

Sewing corners can be great if you want to add pockets, collars, bows, straps, and other decorations to your garment.

This curve and corner serging guide will help on how to easily make a clean and even finish for your curves and corners. At the end of the chapter, you will be able to add professional finishing to the garment no matter the shape.

How to serge corners in a fabric

Step 1:

To make it easy for you to sew corners in your garment, you can draw a seam line at the corner using chalk or a removable pen to help you know when to pivot   .

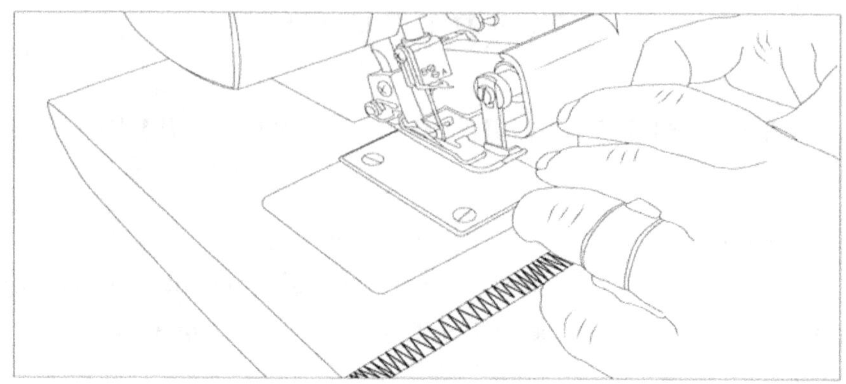

Step 2:

Start sewing along the seam line and slow down your serging speed when you're almost to the corner of the fabric.

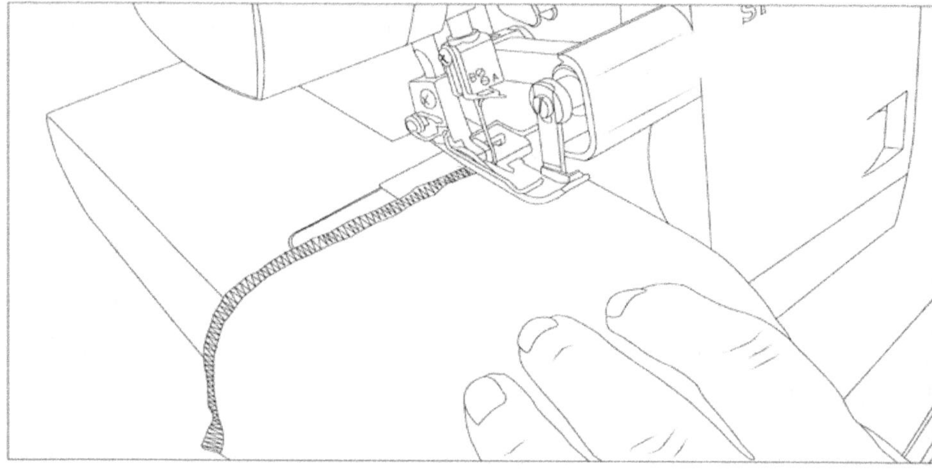

Step 3:

Add one or two stitches past the end of the corner. Let the needle remain down the fabric, and lift up the presser foot and turn the corner of the fabric to face the new direction. Lower the presser foot down and continue serging in that direction.

Step 4:

After sewing the corners, you need to trim and clip your fabric. If there is excess fabric you need to trim it away before you turn the garment on the right side out.

When serging corners of garments, we mostly use the 90 degrees corners. For example, for the corners of pillows, bags, etc. you only need to snip the corners off at 90^0.

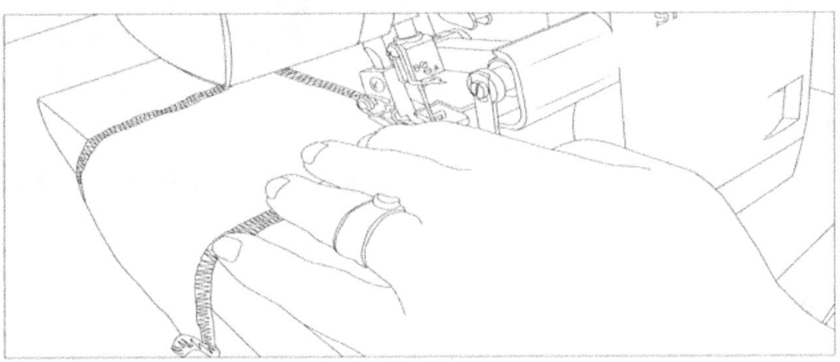

If you have a seam allowance with a width of more than 6 mm (1/4 inch) then you can trim off the sides.

If you're serging on sharp corners like the ones you add on collars, then you need extra trimming of the excess fabric. If the fabric is thick or it has various layers, you may consider grading the seams for better results.

Extra narrow corners

If you want to serge narrow corners, you should consider stitching across the corners several stitches in order to lessen the point. This will result in enough room for seam allowance once you turn the fabric in the right way.

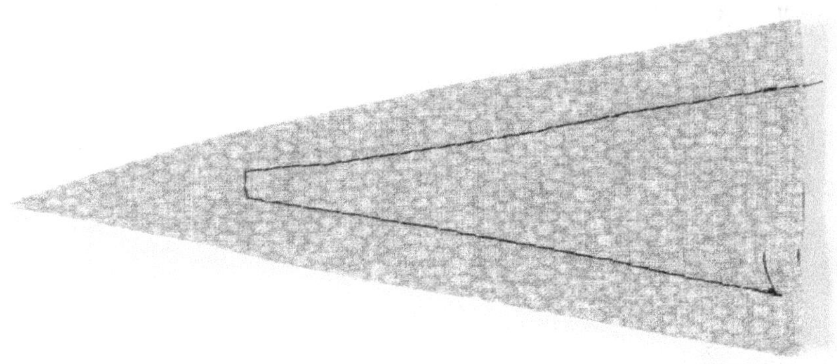

Then trim the excess fabric on both ends to leave a narrow corner.

Inside corners

If you want to add inside corners to the fabric, then you have to snip into the corners up to the stitching line as shown below.

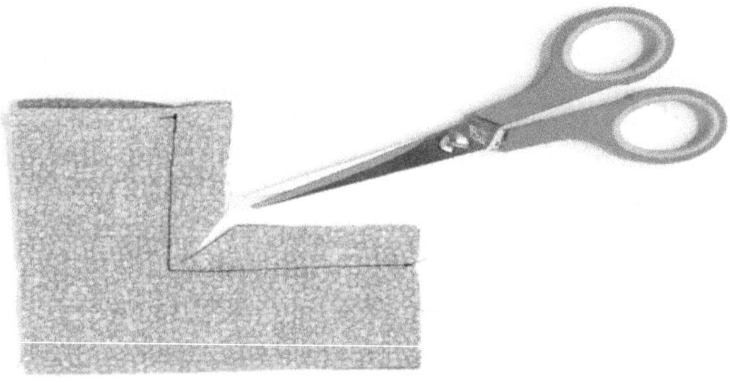

After sewing the corners, you need to turn the corners the right way out. You can use a pointy tool to poke the corners out. Do not use any sharp object because you can accidentally poke a hole or cut the fabric.

Serging mitered corners

You can also serge a 90 degree mitered corner with hems at the edges or a binding. After serging the mitered corner hem, you will not turn the fabric the right way out. Mitered corners are used on items such as napkins, curtains, tablecloths, and quilts.

The corners help reduce bulkiness in the fabric and help and leaves you with flat attractive hems on fabrics.

There are two techniques you can use to serge this type of corner. These techniques depend on whether you will have a narrow hem or wide hem. In a narrow hem method, you will create an opening at the diagonal of the corner. If a wide hem technique is used, then you will shut down the diagonal opening.

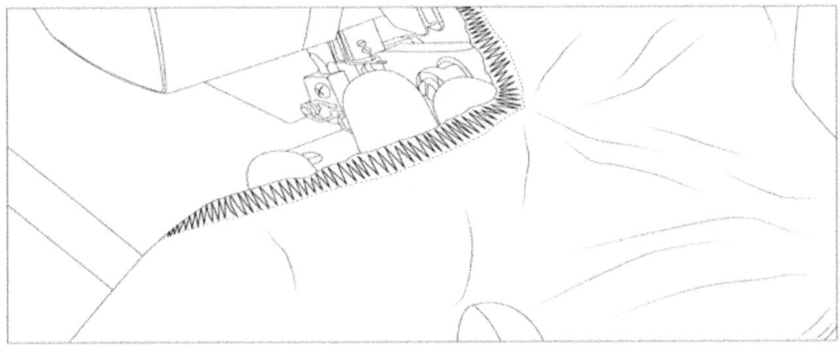

Serging Circle Curves/ Convex Curve

A convex curve is a form of the curve that faces outward just like a circle. This curve is mostly used to sew pockets edges, bag flap, or clutches.

Step 1:

Use the tailor's chalk to mark the seam allowance line that you will follow when sewing. It gives you the accuracy of the curve. Without the drawn line, it makes it difficult to visualize the curved seam and know when to turn so as to sew a perfect curve.

You can use a seam gauge or even a ruler to help you create a few dashes or marks on the fabric then join the dashes together.

Step 2:

Place pins vertically on the fabric to make it easy for you to follow the drawn curve without any interference. The heads of the pins should be left hanging outside of the curve to make it easy to remove them.

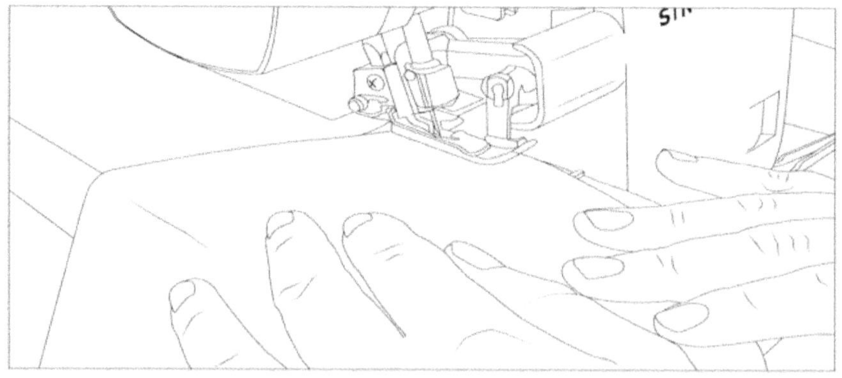

Step 3:

It is now time to sew the curves. First, set your overlock machine to use a small stitch length. You can set a stitch length between 2.0 to 2.5.

Then start stitch slowly. Gently guide the fabric with your fingers and continue serging following the marked seam line.

Step 4:

After sewing all the corners, then you need to trim the excess fabric in order to maintain a smooth curve when you turn the right way out. You can do this by cutting triangle notches from the seam allowance of your convex curve.

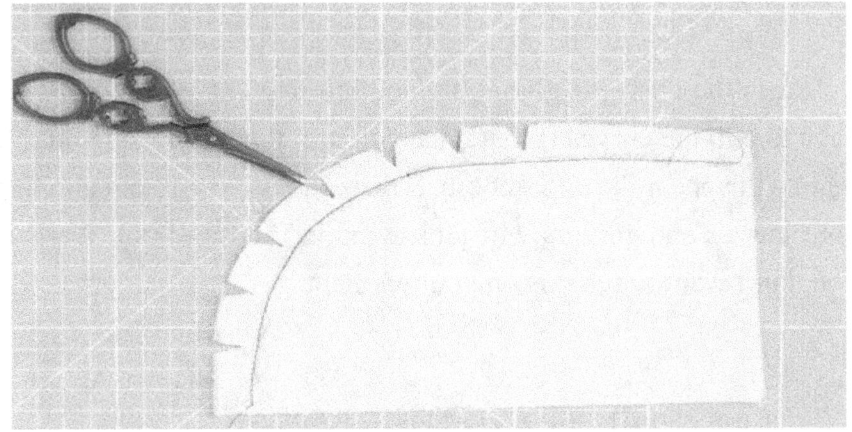

Step 5:
Turn the fabric to have the right side out and then press the curves.

Serging Concave Curves

Concave curves are mostly used in creating necklines and armholes in a garment. You can use the same steps as the sewing convex curve but clipping of the seam allowance is different from that of the convex curve.

Instead of clipping notches in concave, you place snips before the stitch line

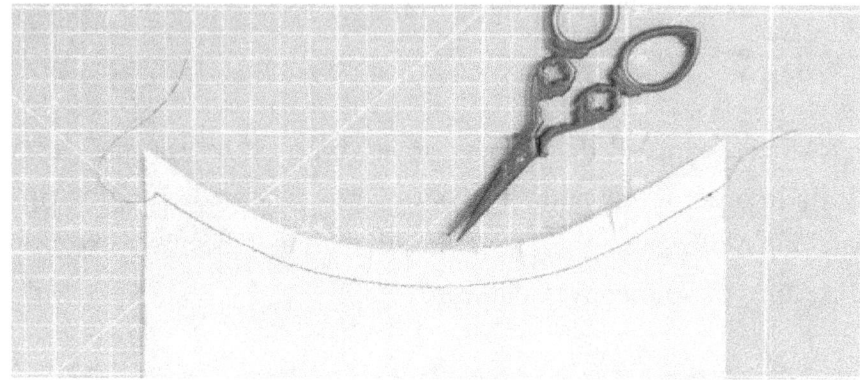

Press the curve to give it a smooth look. The reason why you have to clip the curves is that once you turn them right side out, the seam will appear flat and smooth. If the seam is left without clipping, your curves and corners will look wrinkled and pull out. Am sure you don't want to see this on your garment.

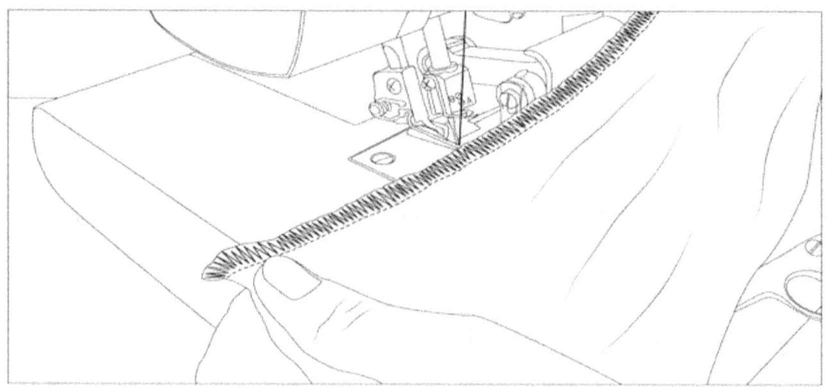

Clipping Curves and Corners

After sewing the curves and corners, clipping them will leave your garment with a professional look.

Clipping is applied to finished projects to prevent them from pulling out strangely or bunching after sewing them. Clipping of corners and curves depends on the fabric shape.

Clipping corners

There are two types of corners: the outward corner and the inward corners.

Clipping outward corners

The edges of your blanket have clipped outward corners. These corners are created by clipping a point diagonally on the seam allowance in order to prevent bulkiness. Then turn your garment on the right side out then use a pointed tool to push the corners out.

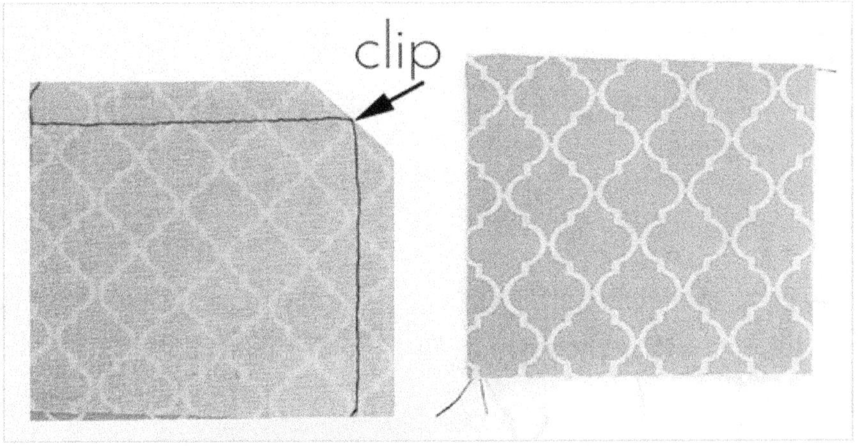

Of the corner of the garment is sharply pointed, you have to trim the excess fabric from the seam allowance for you to have a flat look.

Clipping inward corners

Inside corners are used to make neckline seams. To do this, you need to make a small cut at the corner of the seam allowance. This will make it easy to open up the seam and have a great shape when you turn the fabric the right way out.

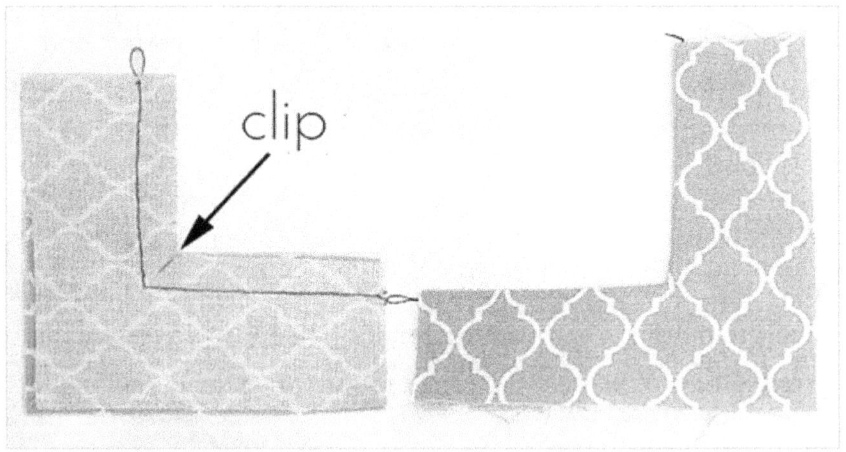

Clipping Curves

Just like corners, you have curves that curve outward and those curve inwards

Clipping convex curves

These mountains like curved shapes can be used to serge necklines, scalloped hems, and other round-shaped projects.

To clip your curved fabric, you need to cut v-shaped notches around the curves. Clipping these curves will eliminate some bulkiness on the fabric when you turn the right way out.

This is because the notch edges will curl up and pack close together to make your garment look flat when turning the right way out.

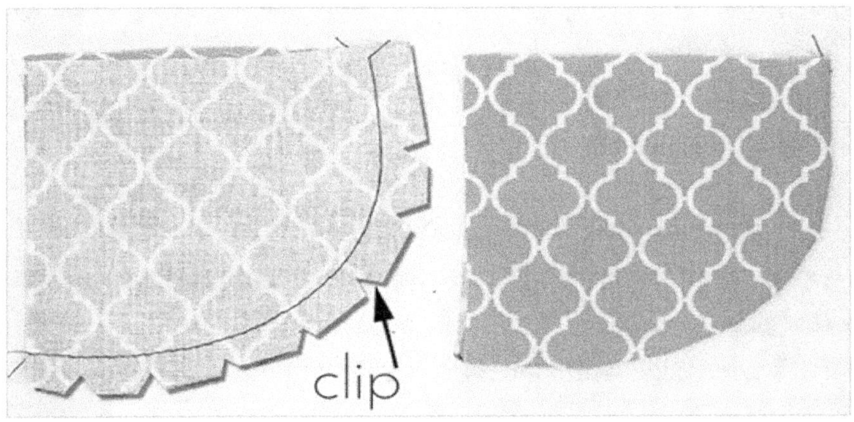

You can use pinking shears to cut the notches faster. These shears cut zigzag edges near the seam line.

Clipping concave curves

When clipping concave curves, you use snips close to the seam line. Be careful not to cut the stitch line. Embroidery scissors can do a faster job of snipping. If you have created a gentle curve then you need less clipping compared to when you have created a steep curve.

After clipping, turn the right way out and press the fabric to have a flat and smooth curve.

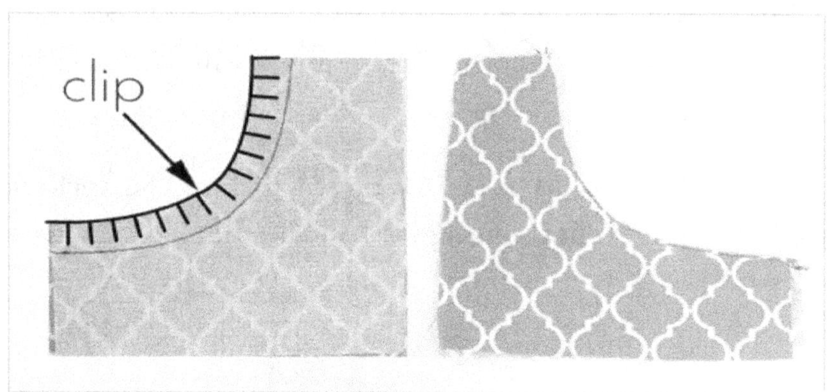

Serging with rolled edges

To create a rolled edge, you only need to have one needle. To use either the right or the left needle depends on whether you want to sew narrow or wide hems. If you use the left needle, you will create a wide edge while the right needle will create a narrow edge.

You should also have your cutting blades engaged to trim the excess fabric and give you a cleaner finish.

Step 1

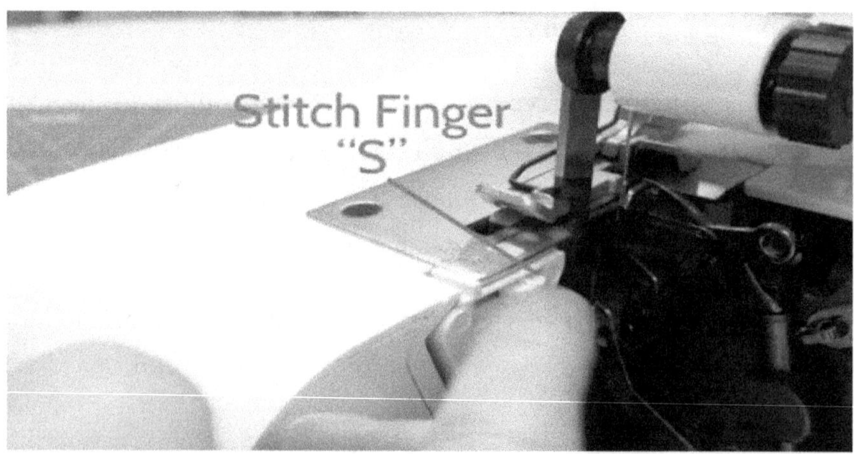

Switch the stitch finger from the standard "S" setting to the "P" setting which is the rolled hem setting.

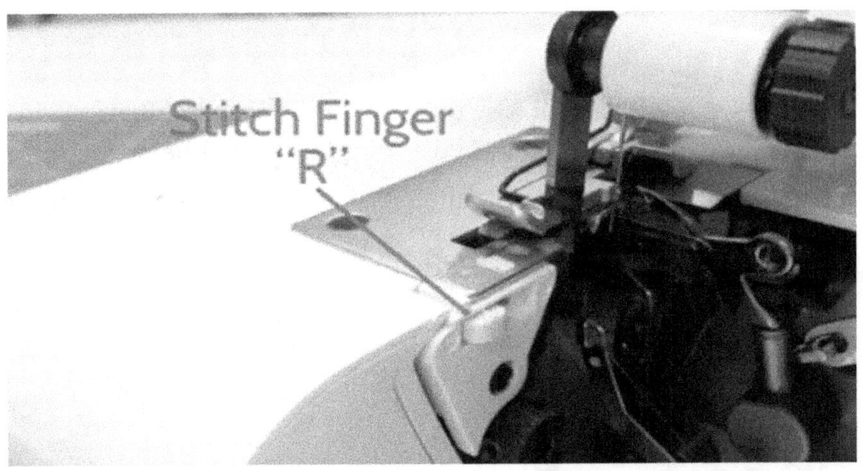

Step 2

Depending on the type of overlock machine you have, you can use a retractable stitch finger to make rolled hems. If your machine doesn't have this feature, you can buy a special rolled hem plate and install it on your machine.

If you're creating rolled edges with 3 threads, you need the upper looper, lower looper, and the right needle.

Adjust the thread tension in order to create the rolling effecting at the edges of the fabric.

Loosen the lower looper so that more thread is allowed into the stitch and also ensure the thread appears on the top and bottom side of the fabric. Increase the lower looper tension to the highest level. Some machines have lower looper tension up to 9 so you can set your machine to use the maximum number in the lower looper tension control and start sewing. Tighten your upper looper thread.

Step 3

Set the stitch length to 3" and stitch width to 4" to create a wider edge using the left needle. As you stitch the rolled hem, the fabric rolls over as you continue stitching. The stitches not only appear on the top side but also they're visible on the hem's bottom side.

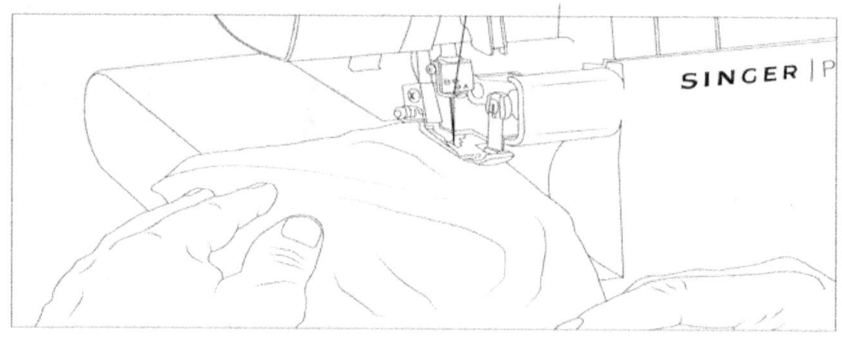

Step 4

Adjust the stitch settings to sew shorter stitch length. A rolled edge stands out when you use a shorter stitch length because a shorter stitch length helps you create a narrow edge with more decorative stitches.

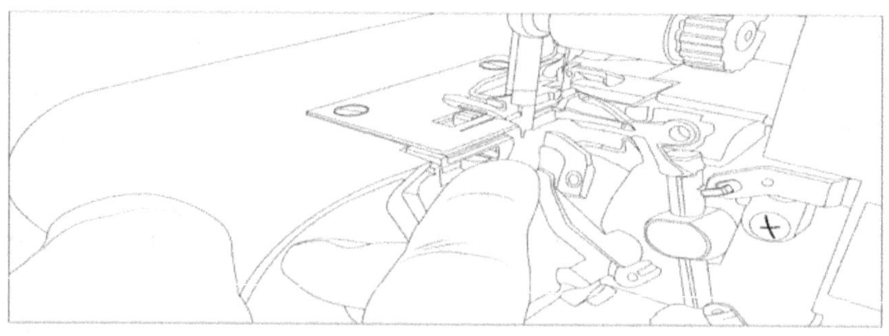

Step 5

Setting a shorter stitch length in your machine will create fuller rolled edges with little space left between the individual stitches. A shorter stitch length uses more thread and looks very cool.

If you use a longer stitch length, then there will be more space between the stitches. Always make sure to have a balance between the stitch length and the tension in order to get better results.

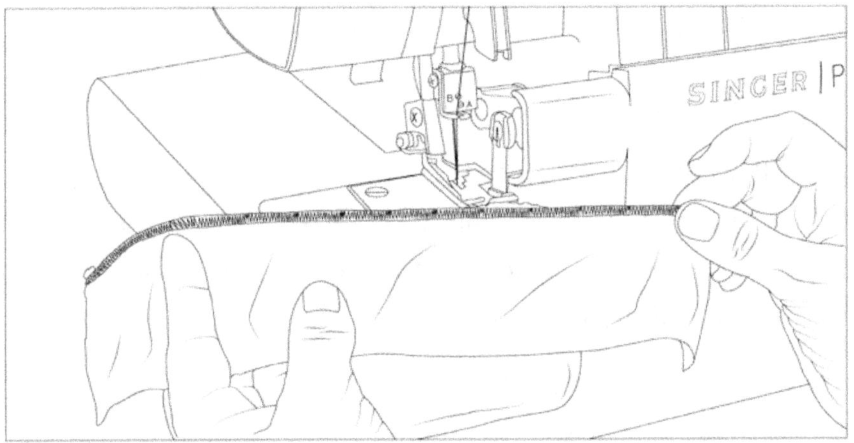

Step 6

If you need to have a narrow hem that is completely covered with no spaces and using the right stitch for your project then you should consider using nylon thread. When you use textured nylon thread for both the upper and lower looper there is no fabric shown between the stitches. This is because nylon thread is thicker and fills in the gaps between threads. When using this thread, you can have a longer stitch length and still get fuller stitches on the fabric.

Step 7

If you need a saddled rolled edge, switch to use the right needle that helps you create a super-thin rolled edge. It also allows you to switch to a narrow 2 thread rolled edge that saves you a lot of thread and reduces the bulkiness of the seam.

Not every machine is 2-thread compatible but if yours is compatible, it should have a 2 thread spreader/ converter which is inserted into the upper looper. Use your serger manual to know how to insert the spreader/converter correctly.

Step 8

With a 2-thread rolled edge, you only use the lower looper and the right needle. While the upper looper is disengaged by inserting the spreader. This will also give you better results just like you're using a 3 thread stitch.

With these two methods, you can easily create rolled edges on your garment and make it look more attractive. It also gives you a clear finishing to the garment. If you don't want your garment to have bulky finishing, you can use your 2 thread converter/ spreader.

Chapter Summary

You can easily add corners and curves to your garments to make them look more attractive. There are different methods of adding the corners depending on whether you need sharp corners or narrow corners. You can also create convex and concave curves that look great and attractive.

After sewing the corners and curves, you have to clip them to give your garment a flat and smooth look. Slipping will ensure you don't have any bulkiness in your garment when you turn the right way out.

With these simple steps, you can make your projects look professional.

In the next chapter, you will learn about Flatlock

CHAPTER SEVEN

Flatlock

So far, we have learned the basics of using an overlock machine. Lets' now dive into more advanced topics.

An overlock machine is used to make a variety of stitches and one of the stitches you can create with your overlock machine is the flatlock stitch.

A flatlock stitch is a type of stitch you can create using either a 3-thread or 2- thread form just like the rolled edges. This type of stitch can be used in a wide range of applications due to its unbulky nature on the finished project. The raw edges of the fabric are encased within the looper threads making the stitches less bulky.

Flatlock stitch is mostly used for hemming activewear garments like stretchy sports clothing, hiking garments, and innerwear. Having a seam allowance inside the garment may chafe athletes' skin.

What are flatlock seams?

In a normal seam, you usually put two pieces of fabric together with the right sides facing each other and then sew along the fabric edges. This creates a flap inside the garment due to the seam allowance used. To avoid this, you can use flatlock seams on your fabric.

In flatlock seams, you put two pieces side-by-side and sew the raw edges of the fabric together. This ensures there is no bulkiness in the fabric.

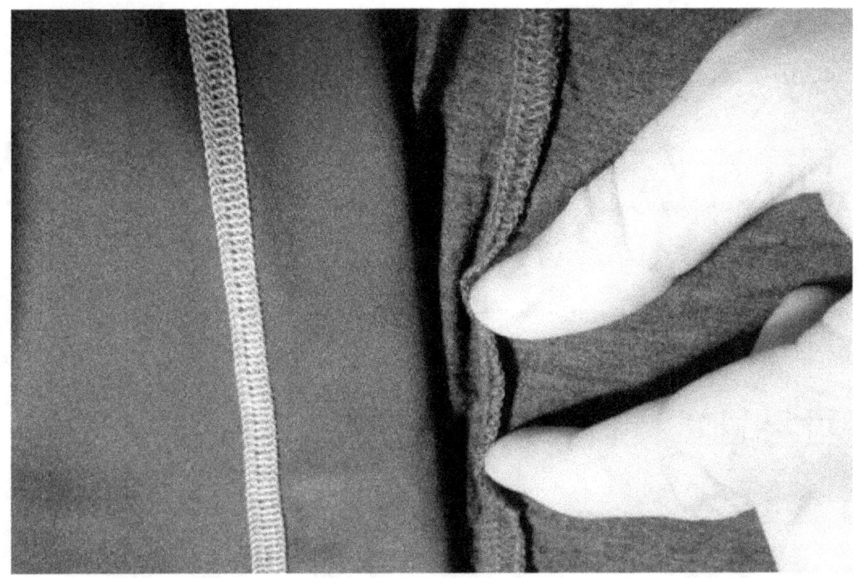

In the above example, the left fabric uses flatlock seams while the second fabric is using normal seams. The flatlock seams don't have any layers left hanging around because the seam allowance is wrapped inside the seam. While the normal seams have seam allowance left hanging around on the wrong side of the garment.

Flatlock seam is suitable for garments worn next to your skin. For example, long-sleeve shirts, t-shirts, pants, gloves, hats, etc. When wearing these garments, they should make you feel more comfortable. You don't need a piece of clothing that causes any discomfort or chafe your skin.

When to use flatlock seams?

Flatlock seams are great for sewing pants and thick garments like fleece jackets. If you use normal seams on these garments, they will be very bulky. The hanging fabric on the inside will also make you uncomfortable and limit your motion.

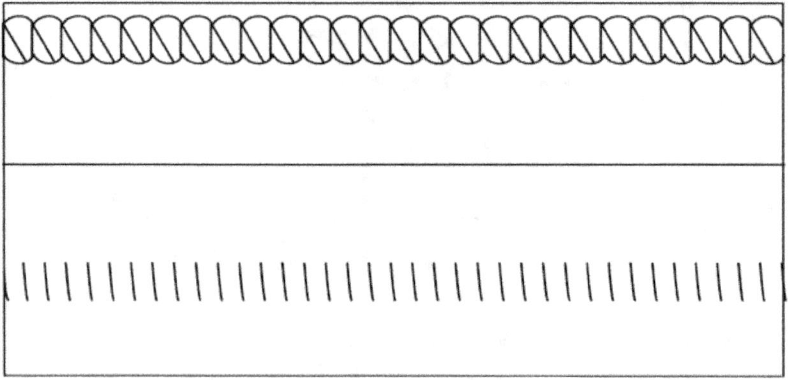

You can also use flatlock seams on base layers made of polyester or nylon fabric. Polyester is very rough and using a normal seam on the material, it will chafe your skin. Further, polyester fabrics have a compression fit and tight fit that presses seams tight against your skin

Two faces of flatlock seams

A flatlock has two sides where the right side of the fabric show stitches that look like a ladder or small bars of threads from the needle thread.

While the wrong side of the stitch displays looper threads as they sew back and forth and create loops across the raw edges on the two sides of the fabric.

If you want the loops to show on the right side of your fabric, then you should sew on the wrong sides together.

Creating these types of stitches looks more decorative. Flatlock stitches on the right side of the fabric can be used to create a blind hem look. However, the wrong side will have stitches that are more decorative. If decorative threads are used then you will have good looking seams.

With these types of stitches, there is no wrong and right side, and the stitches are mostly referred to as ladder or loops (front and back stitches).

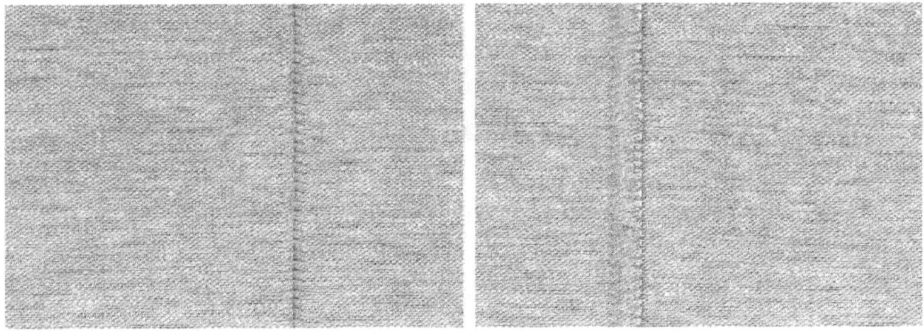

Strength in numbers

The number of threads used to make an overlock stitch correlates to how strong the seam will be. Using a three-thread stitch you will have a strong flatlock seam than when using a two-thread stitch.

When stitching flatlock on high-stretch fabric for sportswear, you should use three-thread stitching. Activewear garment experience a lot of stress and pulling every time, so you need a stronger thread version to support the stretching.

However, if you want to create a hem or a decorative stitch on a loose-fitting garment, then you can use a two-thread version.

Wide vs. Narrow stitches

From our previous topic, we learned that the type of needle you use determines whether you will have a narrow or a wide stitch. Therefore, your needle placement determines the length of your stitches. If you're using the left needle for your stitching, you will create wider stitches while the right needle helps you create narrow stitches.

However, choosing whether to use a narrow or a wide stitch is determined by the thickness or weight of the fabric. Although, sometimes you can choose the stitch width of your preference because the seam is visible and can act as a decorative stitch.

Machine setup

To use flatlock stitches, you need to set up your machine.

Although you can still use a standard serger foot (on the right), it is easy to sew a flatlock seam using an adjustable blind hem foot shown on the left. Ensure you buy a replacement foot that is compatible with the model of your serger machine.

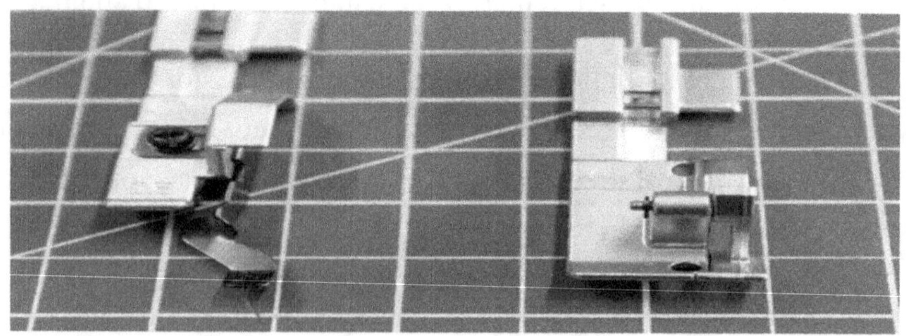

If you're using a standard foot, align the trimmed raw edges of the fabric between the needles.

If you have installed an adjustable blind hem foot in your serger machine, use a piece of scrap fabric to help adjust the slider. Based on the stitches formed, you can decide either to move the adjustable slider to the right or not and tighten the tiny screw on the slider.

When using flatlock stitches disengage the blades because you don't need them. If you leave the blades engaged and you're sewing flatlock stitches on a fold, the blades may cut parts of your fabric. So it is better you be safe than sorry!

When using a flatlock stitch to attach the edges of two pieces of fabric together, you should start by straightening the raw edges of the fabric first to make them even.

Setting up three-thread stitch

You can start by setting up your three-thread flatlock. In this case, you will be using one thread. Use the chart below to adjust your settings.

THREADING/THREAD TENSION SETTING				MACHINE SETUP				
Left needle	Right needle	Upper looper	Lower looper	Rolled hem lever	Upper looper converter	Cutting width	Stitch length	Differential feed
1.5	-	3.5	7	▲	-	6.5	2.5	1

After stitching, you may not notice anything unusual but when you pull the two-layer of fabric, the ladders of the stitch are well exposed while the loops lie flat on the other side.

Three-thread flatlock uses more thread and usually sew strong seams

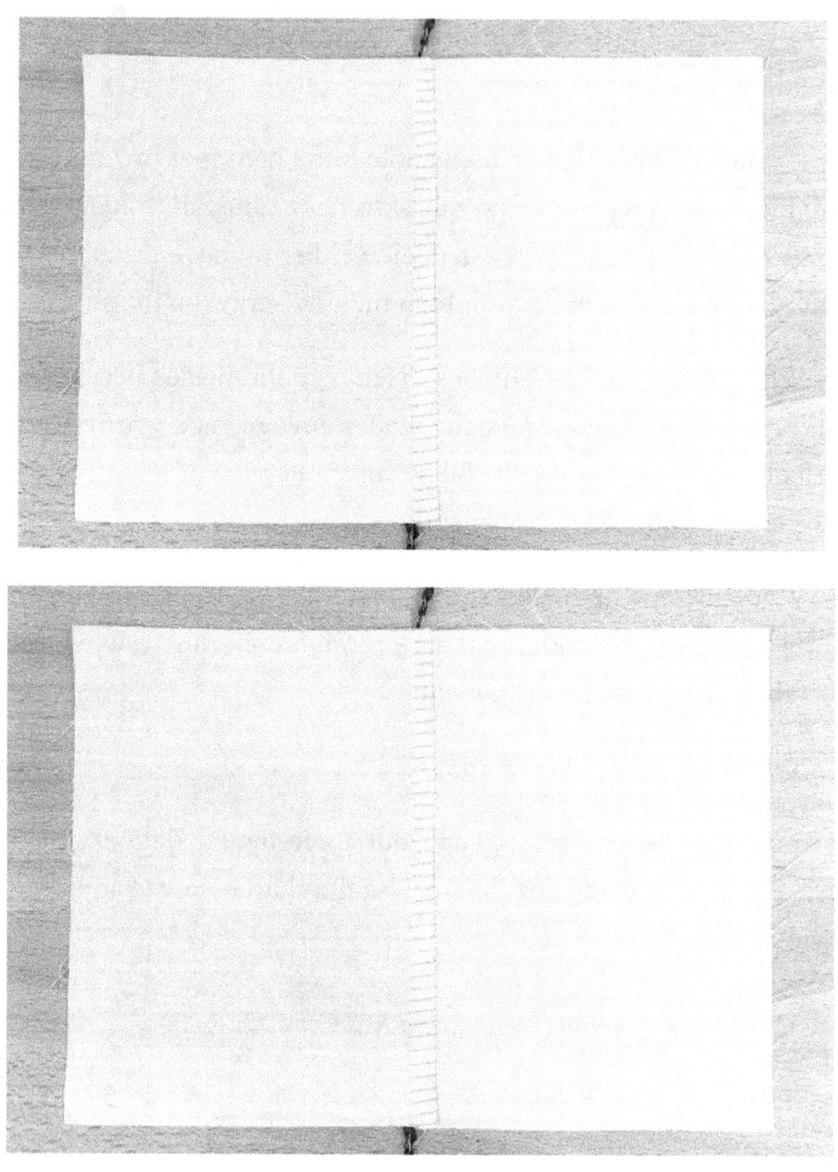

Setting up two-thread stitch

If you want to use a two-thread flatlock, adjust your machine to have the following settings.

2-thread flatlock sews weaker seams compared to the 3-thread flatlock. It also uses less thread.

THREADING/THREAD TENSION SETTING				MACHINE SETUP				
Left needle	Right needle	Upper looper	Lower looper	Rolled hem lever	Upper looper converter	Cutting width	Stitch length	Differential feed
2	-	-	4	▲		6.5	2.5	1

With a two-thread flatlock, you need to install a snap-on upper looper converter (ULC). Different models of overlock have a different snap-on converter so check your manual.

The converter tool stores the looper door when you open the machine. You only slide the blunt end of the upper looper converter into the groove at the top.

Ensure the pointed end is carefully pulled at the back of the looper and hooks through the looper eye.

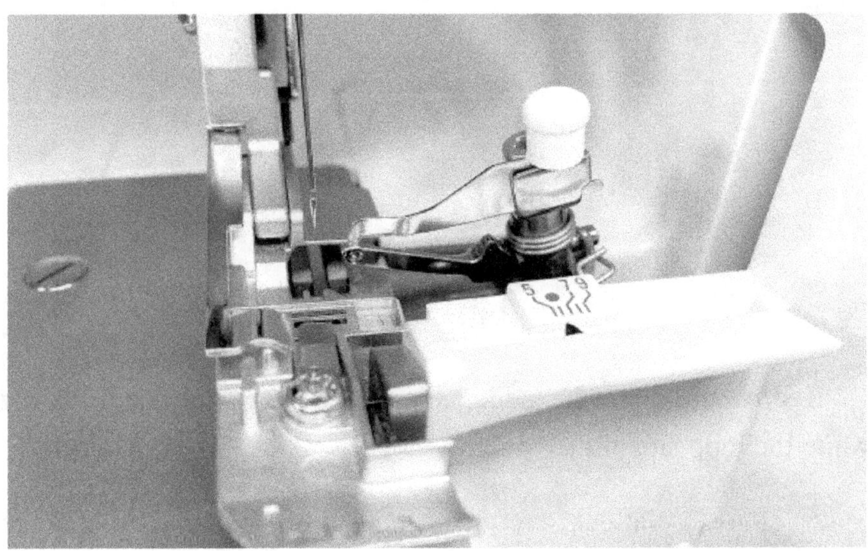

Now stitch the raw edges of the fabric together and then pull the fabric apart to see the difference between your thread-thread stitch and the two-thread stitch. A three-thread stitch adds extra strength to the seam.

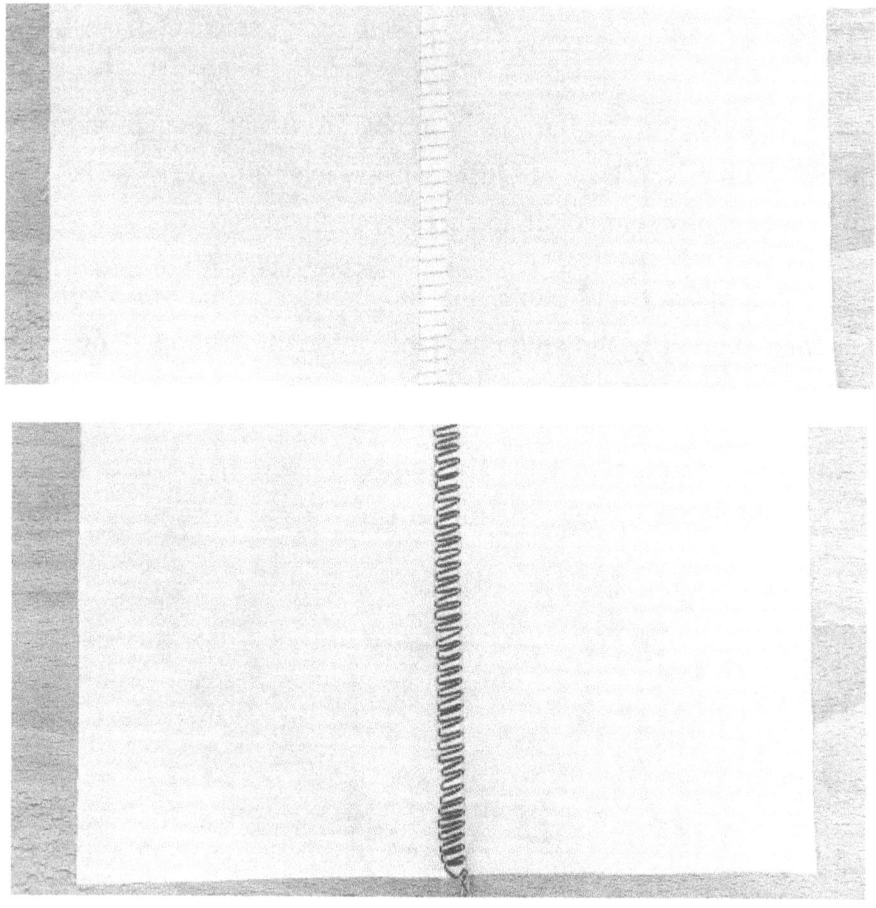

Keep in mind that the ladder side is made using the needle thread while the loop side uses loopers.

A 2-thread flatlock can create both narrow and wide flatlock seams depending on the type of needle you're using.

To get a perfect flatlock seam, you need to test several settings and adjust different controls to give you a perfect stitch. You can practice with a 3-thread flatlock and have a balanced tension setting, and inspect the stitch formation. Change your tension setting and test the stitch. Compare the results of the flatlock seams.

Do that until you come with a perfect stitch for your project.

Hemming with a Flatlock

Another way you can use flatlock stitches is by hemming especially if you want to create an invisible hem. If you use a matching color, the ladder stitch on the right side of the garment will almost disappear. Alternatively, you can use contrasting color threads to form a decorative stitch.

But what is important is how you're going to hem your garment and at the same time, leave it with a professional finishing on the inside.

This can easily be done using the blind hem foot but you can also use your standard foot.

How to create hems with flatlock

1. Fold the fabric with the wrong side to create the hem width and press the fold
2. Fold again and align the folded fabric above the raw edge
3. Serge along the edges using a flatlock stitch. You can use either 2- thread flatlock or 3-thread flatlock.
4. Unfold your fabric and pull it to reveal the set stitches with a lovely inside hem.

If you're using a matching thread, you will have well-blended stitches on the fabric that are almost invisible. But if you're using the contrasting thread color, you will see the threads. Pull the fabric to clearly see the decorative loops.

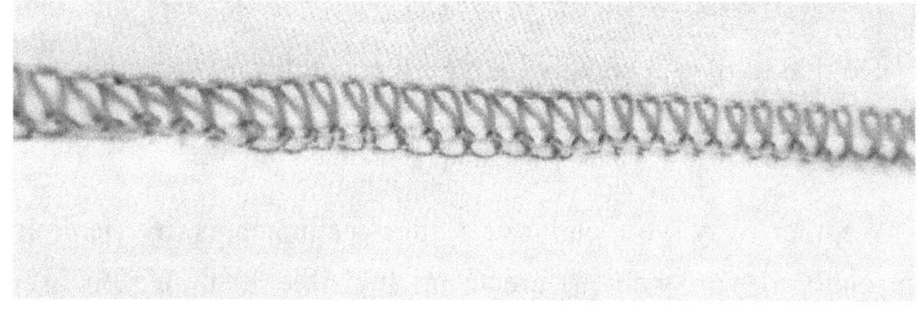

Slightly pulled fabric

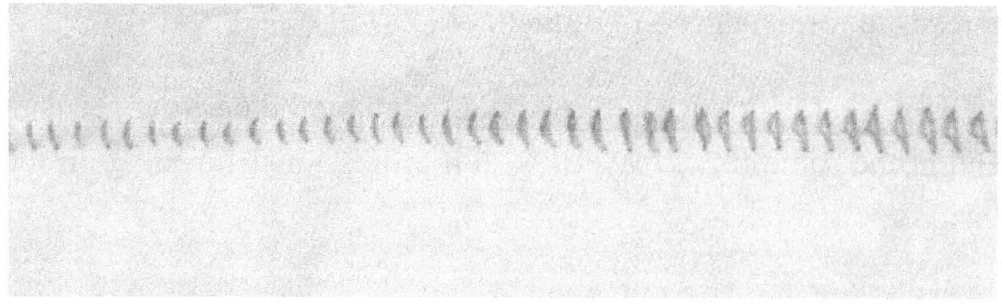

For example, this t-shirt picture below has flatlock seams around the arms that not only adds decorations to the t-shirt it also makes you feel comfortable. The t-shirt also has hems on the sleeve.

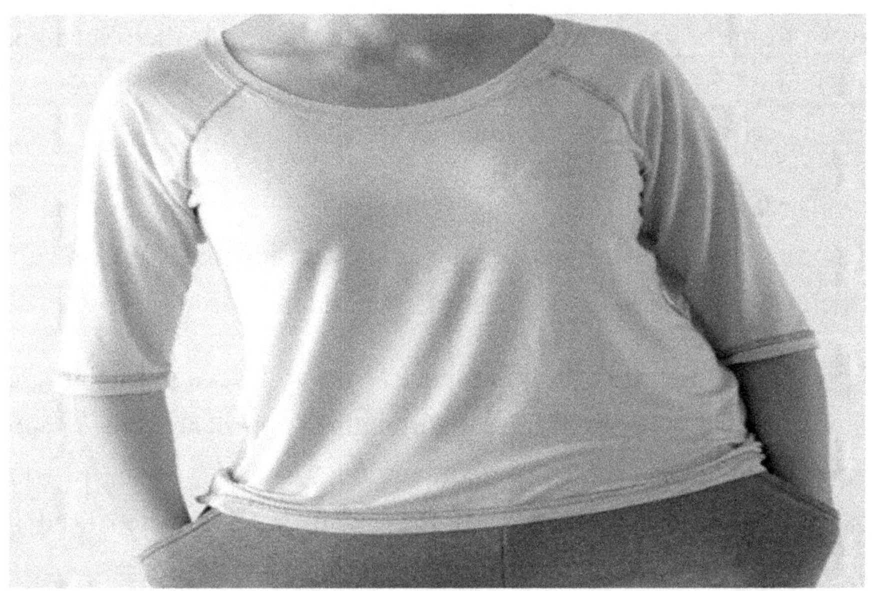

After serging flatlock seams on your garment, you need to secure the ends of the seams. Flatlock seams do get opened up, so it is important to leave at least 3" to 4" thread chain at the start and end of the seam.

You also need to tuck the threads and secure them using a fray blocker.

Troubleshooting Flatlock stitches

When using flatlock stitch, there are few factors you need to consider. For example, the above stitch chart can be found in your serger manual but you can tweak the settings. If the fabric doesn't open up or lay flat, you can reduce the needle tension. As a result, you will have more slacks on the ladders.

In addition, you can adjust the Micro Thread Control (MTC). Increasing the MTC number and moving the stitch finger further away from the fabric helps create an extra room for the seams and the fabric will open up neatly. And at the same time, it will preserve the integrity of the flatlock stitch and tension.

Threads with different weights and textures are great for creating decorative stitches in your garment. The threads give better results when used on the loopers rather than on the threads.

If you use textured nylon threads, you will have extra soft and fluffy seams for your activewear garments. You can also try metallic threads on both loopers to get an extra sparkle seam in your garments. Heavyweight threads form both stitches when used in cotton or wool fabrics.

Chapter Summary

A flatlock stitch is used on stretching fabrics to create a flat seam on both sides of your garment. It also adds some decorations to your garment when different thread colors are used.

Flatlock seams are mostly used in activewear, underwear, or use it on t-shirts to make them more comfortable.

When creating the flatlock stitch, tension adjustment determines the type of seam you will have in your garment. Always confirm with your manual before making the adjustment of the tensions.

In addition, to get a perfect flatlock stitch, you need to practice with scraps of the fabric and adjust the width and tension appropriately.

In the next chapter, you will learn how to use the yarn application foot.

CHAPTER EIGHT

Yarn Application Foot

Yarn application foot is a great presser foot tool that works as an all-purpose narrow cord foot because it can attach any small cord that measures 6 mm wide or less. The foot is mostly used to attach a clear cord to your machine and create a curly finishing line hem.

A yarn application presser foot is also great for attaching a decorative cord, an elastic thread, creating rolled hems, attach beading wire, and also shape the edges of your garment.

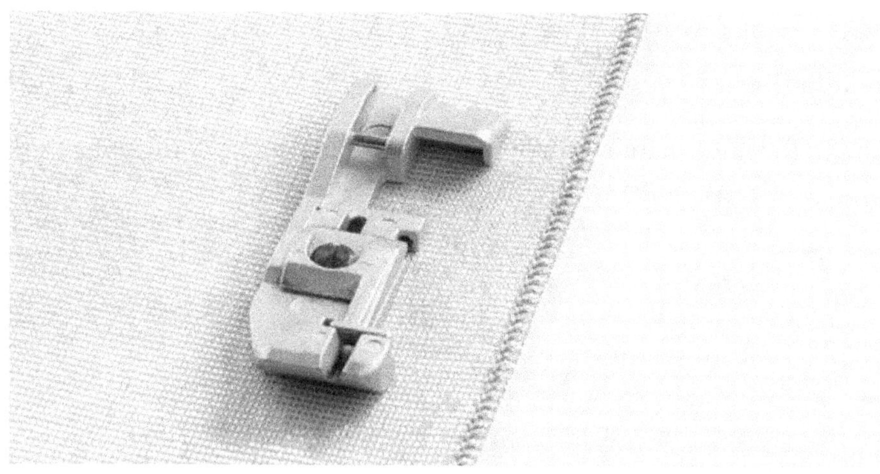

The foot can sew yarns such as cords and nylon gut with a thickness of up to 1.0 mm. The yarn can also create stiffer hems found in a wedding dress or in a valance.

Machine set up

- Set up the right needle in your machine

- You can decide to use any of the two stitch types: Two thread lower looper thread with a wrapped rolled hem or use a three thread upper looper thread with a wrapped rolled hem

- Set the stitch length to 2 mm

- Use normal position for differential feed lever

- Set your upper knife into a working position

Using yarn foot

Remove the standard pre-installed presser foot and replace it with the yarn application foot. Loosen the screw on top of the foot to remove it and screw your yard foot.

The foot applies a narrow cord so well because of the small hole at the front and the little tunnel that feeds through your serger.

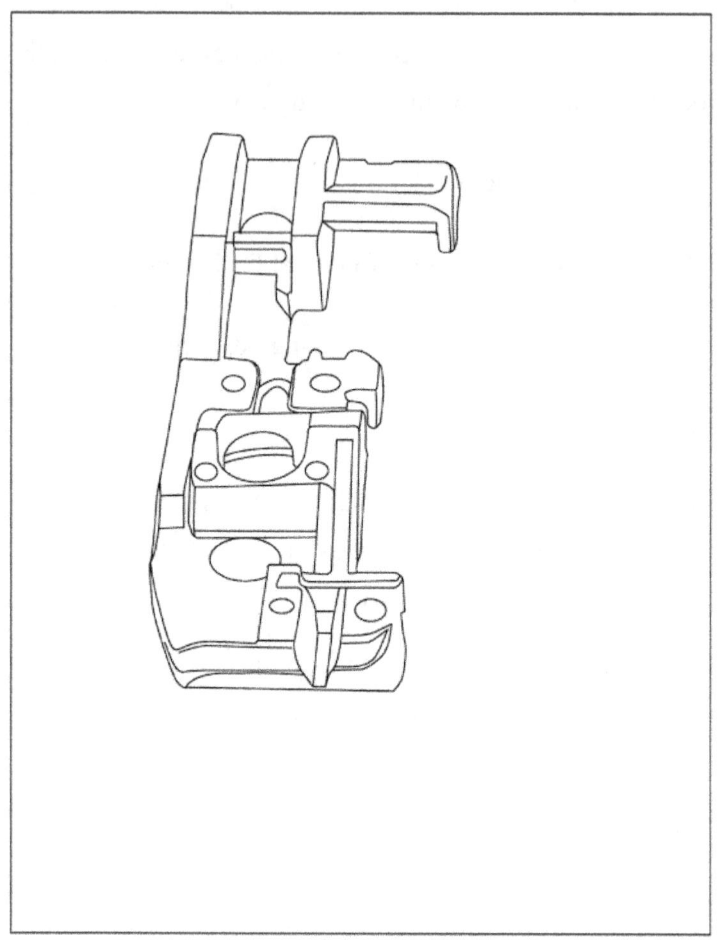

The adjustable screw allows you to adjust the cord. Unscrew it to give you more room to work with.

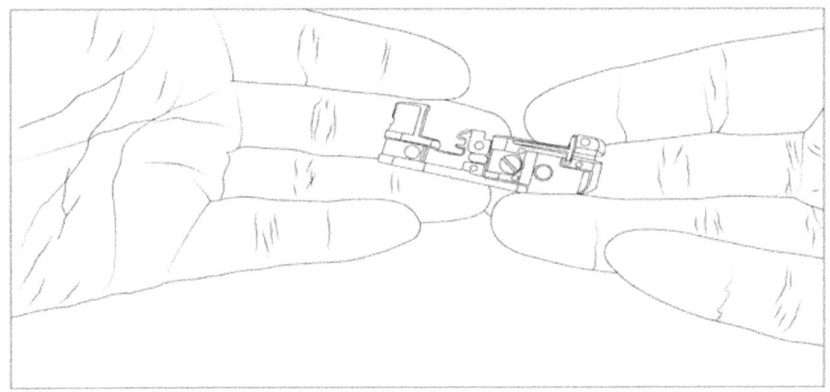

Before you start sewing, you need to thread the cord or your nylon gut. Pass your cord through the front, secure it on the tunnels, and tighten the screw.

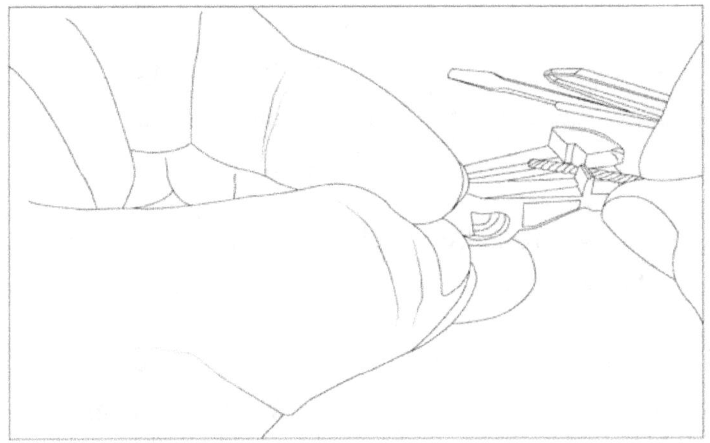

Once you install the yarn foot in your machine, it is very easy to insert a thin clear cord into your machine.

The clear cord can be used to make curly finish lines or bold rolled edge hem to your garments.

For example, let's pick your clear thick finishing line cord that weighs 30" and insert it through the foot and pull the cord to the back.

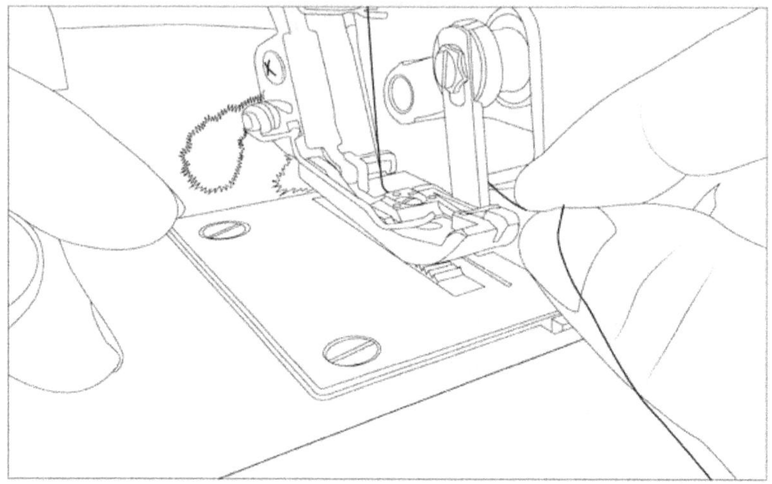

Place a scrap fabric under the presser foot and test the flatlock stitch. If your stitches are perfect, you can now start using your yarn foot.

Start serging a rolled edge chain. Place your fabric underneath the foot and start serging.

When using a thicker cord like the above 30 weight, you have to pull the rolled edge chain at the back to secure the embroidery on your machine and continue serging.

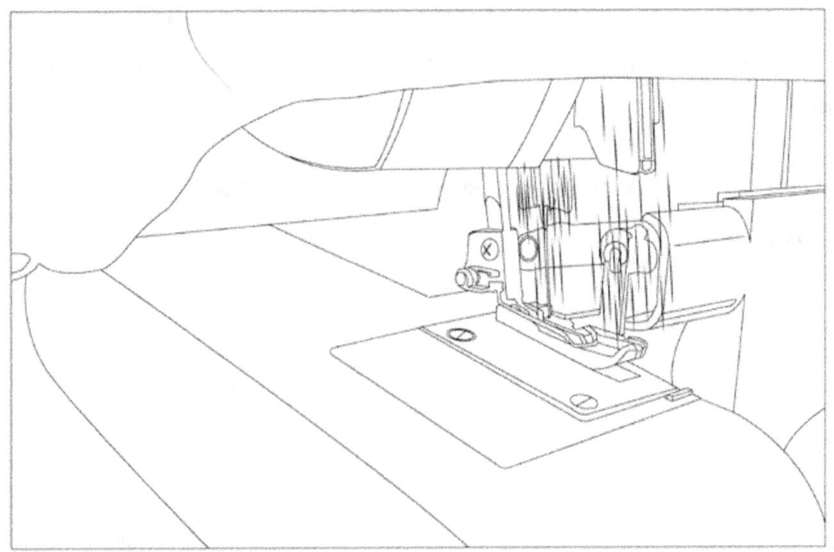

The foot ensures that the cord is stitched at the edge of the fabric and don't have to worry about the cord being pulled by the machine or getting into the knives. It ensures the fabric feeds through well.

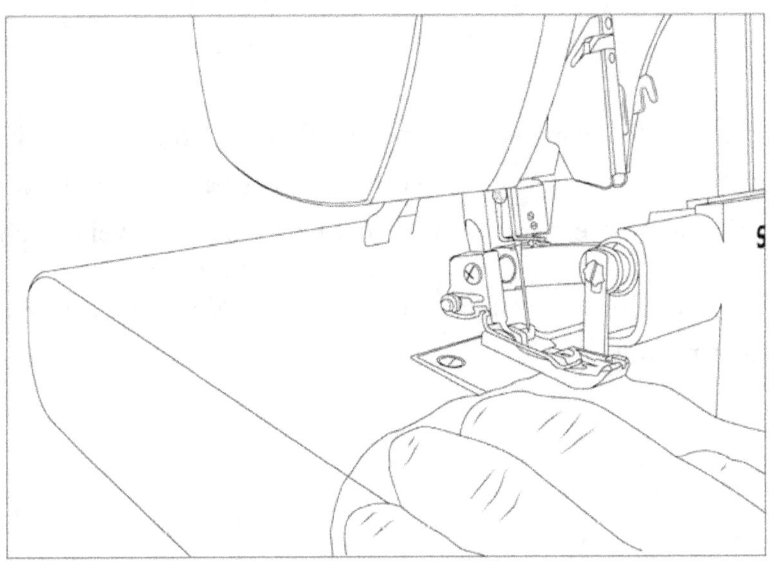

If you need super tight cords in your fabric, wrap the finishing line around a small cylinder and heat it up with your hairdryer or heater.

If you use a nylon thread on the upper looper, you get a super soft finishing.

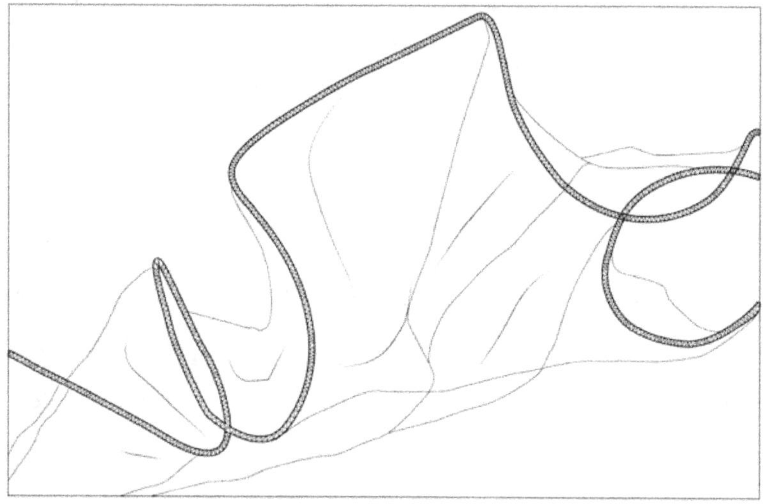

The yarn foot can use any type of nylon cord to give you different sewing effects. For example, you can use a bead stringing wire or jewelry wire to create custom narrow hems to a lightweight fabric.

You can also use a super craft beading cord to give your edges a unique finishing.

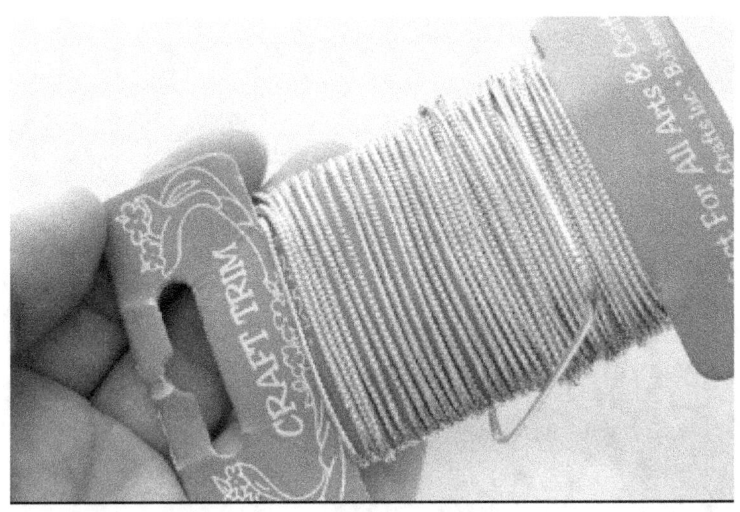

This craft code gives your garments a more decorative look. You only have to thread the metallic thread on the upper looper to get the sparkles on your garment.

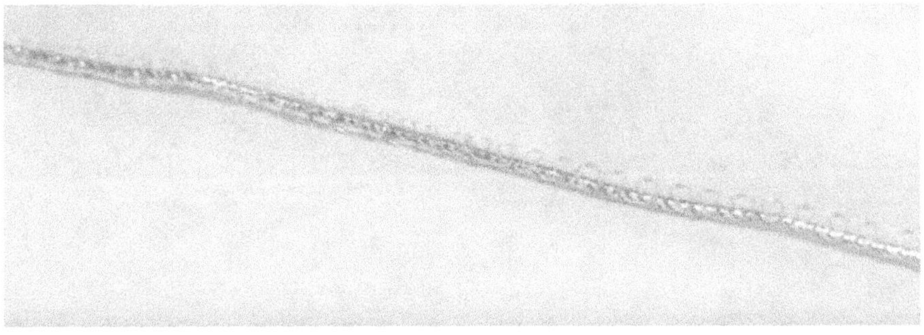

Alternatively, you can use elastic thread to add decorative stitches.

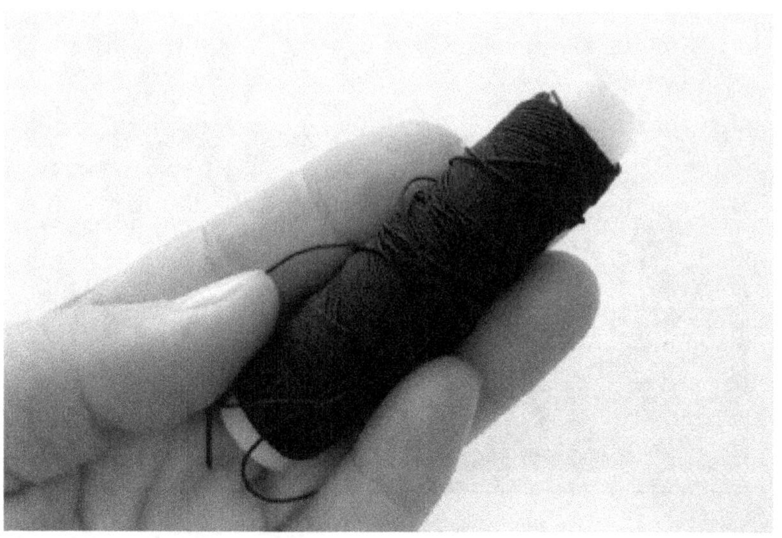

When feeding it through the machine, hold the thread tight with your fingers. This ensures the tension creates a nice gathering on the fabric.

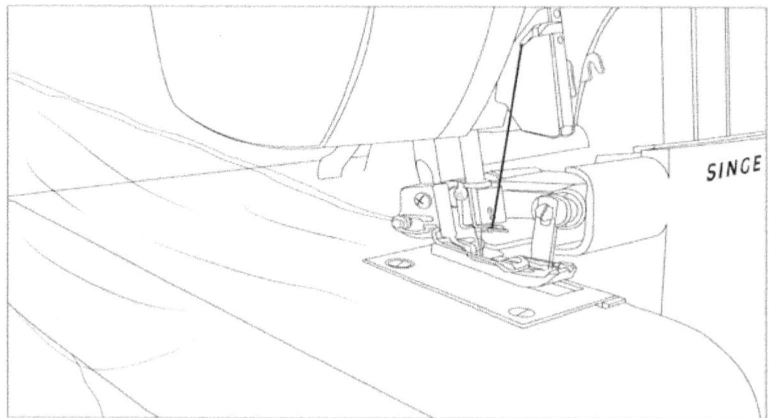

The foot also ensures the fabric feeds well and creates neat gathers for you.

With these easy steps, you can use your yard foot to create decorative stitches with different types of threads. The foot is used to attach a decorative cord, use an elastic thread, or even use a beading wire to make unique curly finishing line hems.

121

Chapter Summary

A yard application foot is an all-purpose foot that you can use to apply a small narrow cord with a width of less than 6mm. the foot can be used to insert clear cord, elastic thread, and beading wires.

With this foot, you can create rolled hems, creating curly finishing lines, adding decorative stitches, and shaping the edges of your garment.

Change your machine to use the yard foot and adjust the machine setting to the desired stitch length and tension. You can set up your machine to use either the three-thread stitches or use the two-thread stitches. Feed the threads to your loopers and needle then start your sewing project.

Yard foot allows you to add professional clean and curly finishing to your garments.

In the next chapter, you will learn how to use lace application foot.

CHAPTER EIGHT

Lace Application Foot

A lace application foot is a great tool that allows you to attach lace trims of different sizes to the raw or finished edges of your fabric. This foot uses a protective built-in guide that keeps the knife away from your lace edges.

The foot consistently feeds the fabric such that it doesn't shift out of place when serging.

It also allows you to create lace to lace trims using your flatlock seam. You can also use lace application foot to add decorative stitches to your fabric and ribbons. The foot comes with a screw you can use to adjust your stitches and allow you to work with a variety of trim sizes.

The lace application foot is an exclusive serger foot that helps you serge delicate trims on a piece of fabric without interfering with the header of the trim.

The adjustable foot ensures you have accurate trims and the lace remains intact. In the end, you will have a professional look and with your exact style.

It provides you with better visibility when attaching a ribbon or a lace to your fabric.

Anatomy of lace foot

There are different lace application foot in the market, but they all work the same way. Therefore, make sure you buy lace foot that is compatible with your serger model. You can check your manual to learn more.

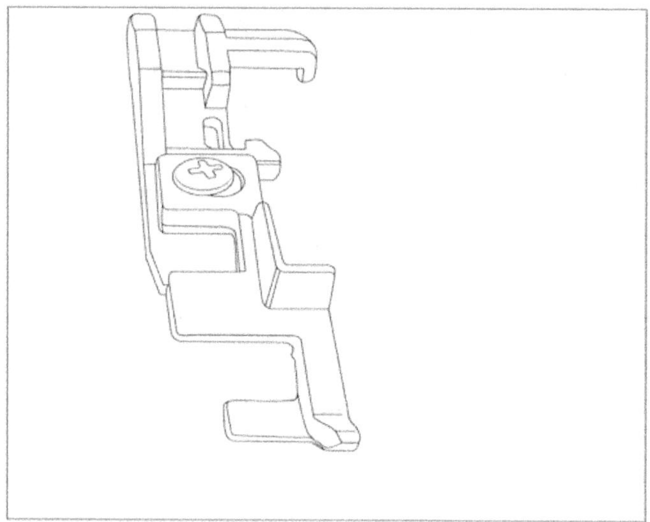

The lace application foot has a long toe that acts as the edge guide for the lace. When you attach the lace to the edge of the fabric, the lace passes through the toe guard at the back of the foot and over to the metal lip.

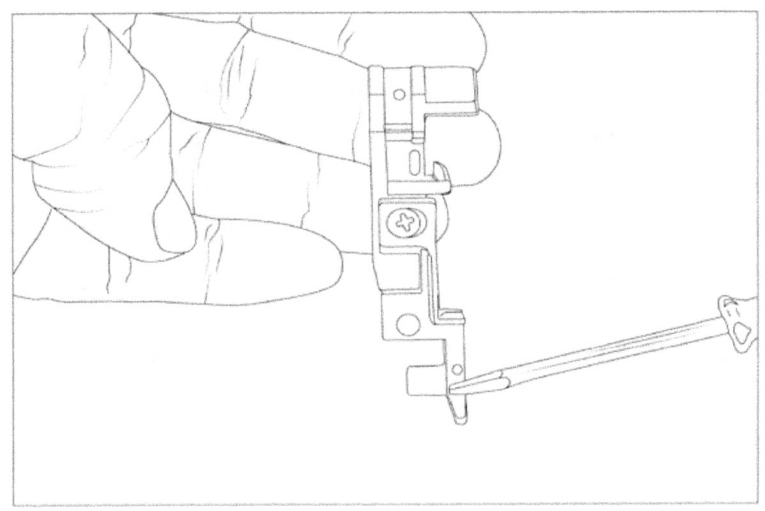

Your fabric will pass through the metal clip unto the front of the lace. This application foot has a screw that you can use to remove the guide but the screw is not adjustable so you shouldn't mess with it.

The lace foot has grooves on the backside that helps feed fabric and lace as you serge and also holds the fabric in place. You don't have to worry about the trim lace shifting or slip off the foot.

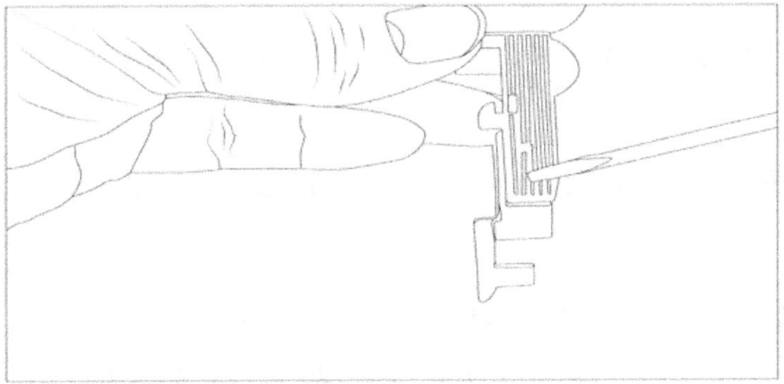

Start serging lace trims

Based on the model of your machine, ensure the machine setting are properly adjusted. In most lace foot applications, needle tension is not required. Although not all serger models have tension control, follow your model manual to know how to adjust the tension if your machine has tension controls.

Depending on the type of model, you can do two-thread flatlock lace or three-thread flatlock lace. In our tutorial, we will focus on three-thread flatlock stitches.

Before you start using the lace foot in your machine, you need to remove the pre-installed presser foot and snap the lace application foot to your machine and start attaching lace.

The lace foot ensures your lace is attached neatly to a raw fabric edge using a three-thread overlock stitch.

Settings

Left overlock needle: use a color of your choice or a coordinating cone thread

Upper looper: use a decorative thread (we will use 12" weight thread)

Lower looper: serger cone thread which doesn't show on your fabrics

Stitch length: 1.5 although you can use varying stitch length based on your preferences, fabric type, and thread weight.

Stitch width: choose the widest

Stitch selector: D

Steps

Take your fabric and place it under the foot.

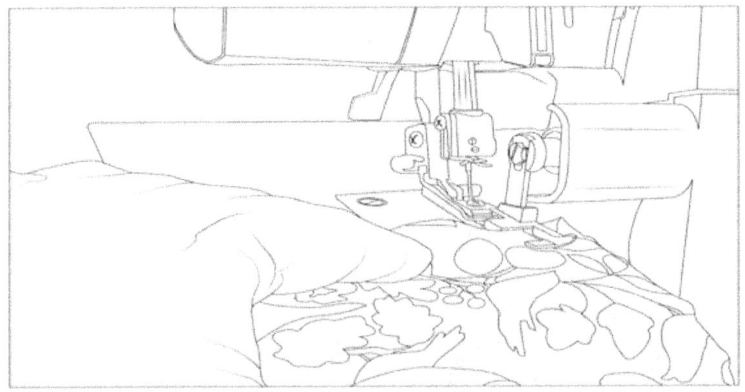

Slide your lace on top of the fabric with the right side down along the guide and start serging.

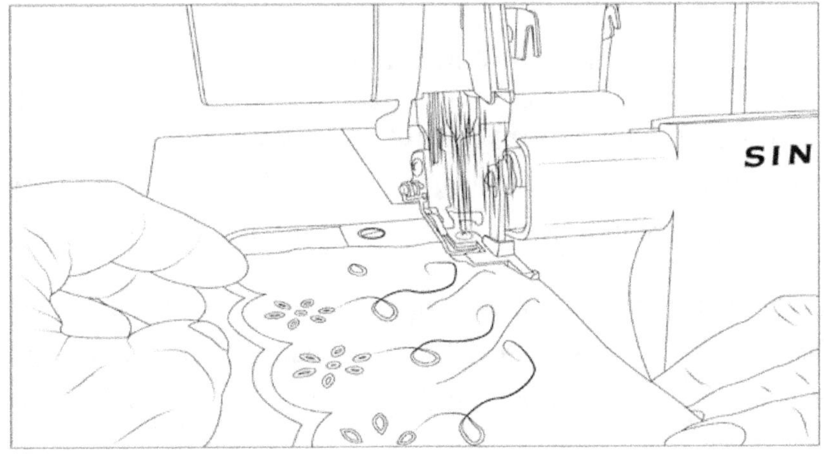

The guide in the metal lip makes your work fast and easier since it makes it easy to control the fabric and the lace from shifting out of place.

It also ensures the lace edges are not cut by the blade as you serge and ensure the fabric feds consistently.

The lace foot ensures your project looks more professional and with neat edges.

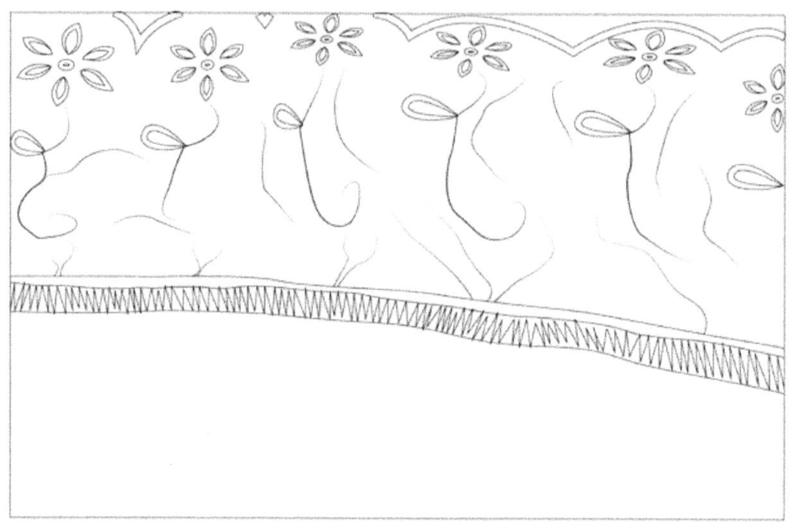

Flatlock stitches with Lace Application Foot

The lace foot is also great for creating flatlock stitches. When you want to join lace to fabrics, you can use flatlock stitches to create unique and decorative stitches on your fabric.

So instead of the fabric passing through the metal lip, insert both fabrics in the lace with the right sides facing each other along with the toe guide and over the metal lip.

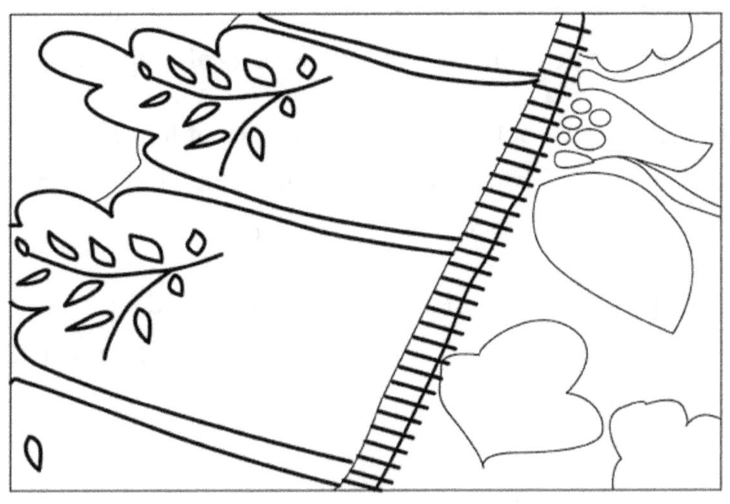

The loops are created over the stitch finger with a seam allowance of about 1/8" off the lacing fabric edge. There is no tension in the needle and sometimes it causes the stitches to appear loose. This is because the upper looper threads are loose while the lower looper thread is tightened. As you serge, the fabric feeds through with ease.

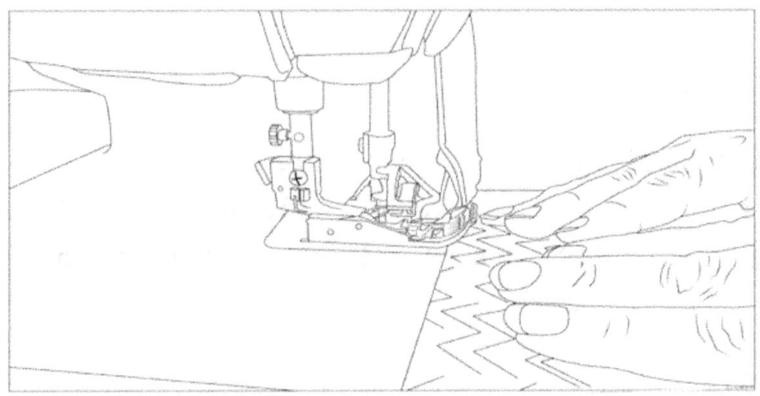

Once your flatlock stitches are formed, you just pull the fabrics, to have a flat and neat finish. Flatlock stitches also appear strong.

The lace foot can help you join two pieces of lace edge together. Place the pieces of fabric through the toe guide and over the metal lip and serge the fabric to the end.

In addition, you can thread your needle with decorative thread and use flatlock stitches on different laces to create a unique finishing to your fabric.

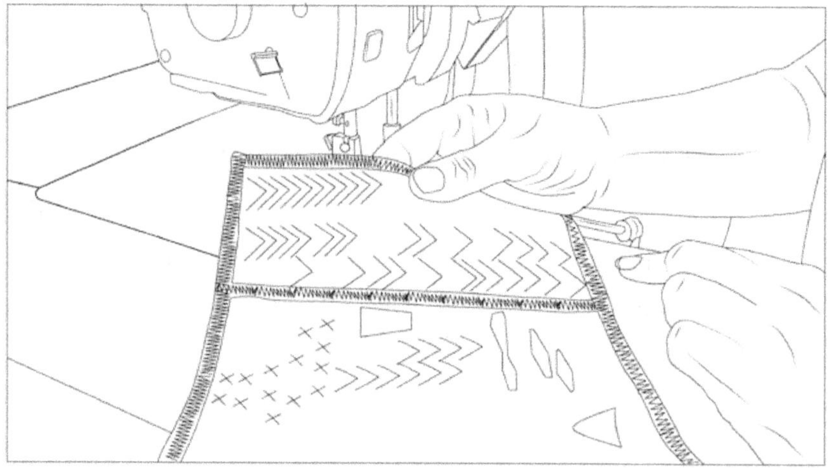

Creating different stitches on your garment makes it look more decorative. You can practice with different types of laces and different threads for your upper and lower looper to make the stitches look unique and neat.

Chapter Summary

Lace application foot is a great tool that allows you to sew flatlock stitches among other decorative stitches in your fabric. The foot has an edge guide that ensures your fabric is put in place as you serge. The guide also prevents the knife from trimming your fabric while stitching.

Align your fabric and the lace with the guide and don't pull it, let the foot feed the fabric through. Depending on the model of your machine, you may have different lace applicator foot but they all serve the same purpose. You only need to master the settings of your lace foot from the instruction manual of that model.

When sewing decorative stitches, you consider having different thread colors and weights. adjust the stitch length based on the fabric and serge your fabric. After serging, pull the pieces of the fabric so that you have a flat seam on your garment. Needle stitches on the right side out should appear clean and neat.

FINAL WORDS

This step-by-step instruction guide helps beginners to know how to operate a serger machine. The manual introduces you to different parts of a serger machine and what you need to know about them. If you need to have a professional finishing to your garment, a serger machine will help you achieve that.

In our introduction chapter to sergers, we are able to learn what a serger machine is and what makes it different from a sewing machine. You're also able to learn different parts of the serger machine and their functions.

The serger machine is also known as the overlock machine creates seams to your fabric and at the same time, it trims excess fabric. This makes them faster in sewing garments as well as gives you a clean finishing. The machine performs multiple functions simultaneously to create a strong stitch.

After knowing the different parts and functions, you're also able to learn some of the tools you need in order to get started with your serger machine. These tools are a must-have for you to successfully complete your sewing projects.

These tools enable you to set up your machine and get it running. For example, knowing the needle parts makes it easy to fix the needle in your machine and also how to thread it. In this chapter, you're able to learn how to choose the best serger machine. We are able to evaluate the factors to consider before making your buying decision. In addition, we listed some of the best Serger machines in the market you can choose based on your needs.

In chapter three, we learned how to thread your machine like a pro! With the step-by-step guide, you are able to thread both the left and right needles and both the lower and upper loopers. You are also able to know how to adjust the needle tensions and differential feed for you to have a perfect stitch.

Learning how to customize the serger controls helps you adjust the stitches that give you better results based on the type of fabric you're using. Further, you are also able to know how to troubleshoot any threading issue with your machine and fix it.

Once you have threaded your machine, it becomes very easy to change the threads. With just a few steps, you can easily change the threads to match your fabric. You don't have to follow the long procedure of threading your machine again. Your secret trick is to cut the old thread and replacing it with the new thread. All you need is to tie a knot of the old thread with the new thread.

A serger threading and thread tension differ from that of your regular sewing machine. Thus you need to know how to operate and adjust them. In a serger machine, the knives trim part of the seam allowance as you stitch your fabric. And for that reason, you need to know how to guide your fabric under the presser foot and what to expect while stitching. Once you're comfortable with how your machine operates, you can dive in for your first sewing project.

There are different types of stitches you can create with your serger machine, That is why in chapter 4, you're able to learn how to use different types of stitches to add finishing the raw edges of the fabric, create decorative stitches, blind hem stitches, rolled hemstitches, and other forms of stitches.

You're also able to learn how the stitches are formed and when to use each type of stitch. The type of stitches to use and how to use them depends on the model of the serger machine you have. Some models come with a built-in serger foot that allows you to create different types of stitches while others require you to purchase a particular serger foot designed specifically for doing a particular stitch. Read your serger manual to know more about what type of stitches you can do with your machine.

When you choose a particular stitch for your fabric, you have to determine the number of threads to use (1- thread, 2-thread, 3-thread, or 4-thread), whether to use the left or the right needle and how to set up the loopers.

Sometimes, depending on the stitch you choose, you have to change the presser foot, change the needle position, adjust the tension dials, and disengage the blades. Learning how to create a balance between the loopers and the needle threads helps create a perfect stitch. Confirm with your manual before making any changes to your serger controls.

The fabric type affects how the stitches are formed and that's why we have learned how to adjust the tension dials and stitch length to have a clean stitch. However, there are instances where adjusting the tension can not balance your stitches. In such instances, you need stabilization of seams so as to improve the quality and strength of your seams. In this tutorial, you're able to learn how to stabilize your stitches using stay tape, ribbons, binding, and using clear elastic.

Stabilization of seams helps reinforce stitches in some of the high-stress areas like your shoulders or when sewing a stretchy fabric and don't want it to warp out of shape. The above simple steps will help you employ different techniques to stabilize your stitches.

In chapter 6, you're able to learn how to serger around corners, and curves. Know how to stitch rounded corners, and other forms of curves make it easy to create projects that have pockets, collars, straps, bows, bag flap, clutches, and other decorative shapes. You are also able to know how to clip the corners and curves to give your garment a professional look.

Further, you're to know how to create rolled edges and flatlock stitches on the raw edges of the fabric and give your projects a neat finishing. Flatlock seams allow you to sew raw edges of two pieces of fabric side-by-side. It is a great stitch for joining fabrics together and leave you with a flat decorative stitch. If you want to create an invisible stitch, you can use the hemming technique with a flatlock.

In addition, we have different thread choices for serging, if you want to make decorative stitches, you have to delve into the world of decorative threading, use yarns, fine ribbons, and beading wires. Different threads are made using a variety of fibers that make them look beautiful and sparkle when used on garments. Using different tools like yarn application foot, lace application foot, and gathering foot among others makes your serging better.

Threading a nylon thread on your upper loopers will give you a super soft finishing on your garment. You can also use bead stringing wire to create custom narrow hems in your garment. A lace foot allows you to attach different lace trims to the raw edges of your fabric. The foot provides better visibility when attaching ribbons or lace into fabrics.

A narrow clear elastic adds stability to your knit seams. If you're using lightweight fabrics or stretchy fabric, then a clear elastic thread will be of great use. Continue practicing with different stitches and make professional custom-made projects.

Image Credit: Shutterstock.com